COUNTER POWER

Making Change
Happen

About the author

Tim Gee works with campaigning organizations to deliver training sessions for activists. He has a degree in Politics from Edinburgh University where he was also active in the student movement. Tim has contributed to several campaigning guides and manuals and is involved in numerous grassroots campaigns. To contact the author, email: counterpowerbook@gmail.com

Dedication

This book is dedicated to Helen who was involved in the earlier days of so many of the movements that I am involved in now. I hope that you would have been proud.

Acknowledgements

The ideas in this book are the product of hundreds of discussions and debates, followed by countless drafts and redrafts. People who have contributed through conversations, comments or criticism include Glen, Anna, Annette, Yvonne, Clive, Mark, Neil, Glyn, Jim, Liam, Adam, Roger, Jesse, Kevin, Danny, Jess, Juliette, Joanna, Sarah-Jayne, John S, John C, Jonny, Jonathan, JJ, Gi, Anthony, Bill, Claire, Colin, Matt, Chris, Phil, Amy, Brittany, Nadia, and Claire's friend Ollie.

In particular, I want to thank: Mama Maria, for looking over every chapter at least twice; Alain, for his watchful eye and playing a part in getting me interested in this stuff in the first place; Paul, who helped refine the concepts; Lucy, who wasn't afraid to make suggestions, from the smallest details to turning it around completely (and was right); Keshav, who went so far as to write a couple of short essays on the chapters I sent through; and Jaimie, who pointed out how a few words out of place could change the meaning entirely.

Any mistakes are of course my own. If there are any I hope they do not undermine my argument.

Credit is also due to all the people at the Working Class Movement Library in Salford who keep that important place going. I recommend a visit. I also recommend a visit to Cafe Pogo and Gorki House in Hackney, London, which, as well as being lovely places, put up with me for hours on end.

Thanks go to my editor Chris Brazier for giving me the opportunity to write this in the first place and for always being constructively honest about his opinions alongside everyone else at New Internationalist and Oxford Publicity Partnership who helped make this possible in different ways.

No thanks go to the Procurator Fiscal of Edinburgh, who took me to court on four different occasions following a gluey piece of civil disobedience against Royal Bank of Scotland's financing of tar sands. The book would have been finished sooner if it hadn't been for you.

TIM GEE

COUNTER POWER

Making Change Happen

WORLD
CHANGING

Counterpower: Making Change Happen
First published in 2011 by
New Internationalist Publications Ltd
55 Rectory Road
Oxford OX4 1BW, UK
newint.org

Front cover design: Andrew Kokotka.

Printed by T J International Limited, Cornwall, UK
who hold environmental accreditation ISO 14001.

MIX
Paper from
responsible sources
FSC
www.fsc.org   FSC® C013056

British Library Cataloguing-in-Publication Data
A catalogue record for this book is available from the British
Library.

Library of Congress Cataloguing-in-Publication Data
A catalogue record for this book is available from the Library
of Congress.

ISBN 978-1-78026-032-7

Contents

Introduction

'Disobedience, in the eyes of anyone who has read history, is man's original virtue. It is through disobedience that progress has been made, through disobedience and through rebellion.'

Oscar Wilde

From my vantage-point in the gallery, the man on the stage is a mere dot in a vast hall filled with people. He opens his mouth to speak:

'I wish you Egypt!'

His voice is almost a whisper but the audience is drawn in. 'I wish you Egypt so you can decolonize your minds, for only then can you envision real liberty, real justice, real equality.'

There is a murmur of agreement.

'I wish you Egypt so you can tear apart the sheet with the multiple-choice question, "what do you want?", for all the answers you are given are dead wrong. Your only choice seems to be between evil and a lesser one.'

He raises his voice in a gentle crescendo.

'I wish you Egypt so you can, like the Tunisians, the

Egyptians, the Libyans, the Bahrainis, the Yemenis, and certainly the Palestinians, shout "No! We do not want to select the least wrong answer. We want another choice altogether that is not on your damned list".'

The hall erupts with applause.

The man is Omar Barghouti: a former resident of Egypt, a leader in the nonviolent struggle for justice in Palestine and a man whose cause is cited by the Egyptian revolutionary who shares the platform as a major source of inspiration. The occasion is a rally in the wake of the resignation of (former) Egyptian President Hosni Mubarak, providing the climax of a day of seminars and debates on people power.[1] It is hopeful, it is buzzing and it is packed.

Following the Arab Spring, revolution is on the tip of everybody's tongue. And it isn't just the usual suspects singing its praises. Even the US academic Francis Fukuyama – famous for having once proclaimed 'The End of History' – has been on television praising the Egyptian Revolution.

This book began as an enquiry into how campaigning might be more effective. But the more I read, the more convinced I became that a successful campaign is an unfinished revolution and that a revolution is the result of a series of successful campaigns.

The project began in April 2009, not long after the leaders of some of the most powerful countries in the world met in London at the G20 Summit. The protests that accompanied their visit were significant. First, 35,000 people from 20 different countries took to the streets under the banner *Put People First*, calling for the democratization of the financial institutions that had caused the most recent global economic crisis. Then, on the eve of the summit itself, a number of different networks took to the streets again, occupying the financial district. The *Put People First* march passed without incident. The day of civil disobedience prompted one of the most brutal police responses in recent memory.

After the G20 had passed, I took a week off work. Spurred on by events, I determined that I should use the time to delve into the archives of history and try to learn from movements past to understand better what makes a campaign successful. My first stop was the Working Class Movement Library in Salford – a monument to the struggles of those who have gone before. It is a stunning collection of badges, t-shirts, pamphlets, books, leaflets, hand-written records and radical newspapers from the 1790s to the present day. Each tells their own story. The building is familiar to me – as a child, I spent many summer days there when my stepfather was the librarian.

The entrance hall was smaller than I remembered but no less impressive. Hung from every banister of the central staircase were beautifully crafted banners. To the left, an early trade union banner, to the right, one from the women's movement. On the next landing up was a banner from a coal miners' strike. To my surprise, dead center was a slightly smudged banner which I had helped to make: a huge bed sheet with the message 'Killing people is wrong – in the USA *and* Afghanistan'. We had used it for a vigil every evening for three months in late 2001.

I pointed out the banner, then explained my mission to the new library manager. She asked how long I had.

'A week.'

She laughed and replied: 'It will take you much longer than that'.

She was right.

It was the beginning of a project that, on and off, would take another two years, leafing through autobiographies, histories, newspapers and pamphlets, all the time cross-checking against textbooks and articles about the nature of power.

What struck me was how almost every major campaigning movement of the past seemed to have the same debates that we are still having today: Do demonstrations make a difference? How important is the sympathy of the mainstream media? Does law-breaking help or hinder campaigning? Is violence ever justified? It even filters right through to the most procedural issues about the appropriate balance between vegetarian and non-vegetarian food at campaigning conferences.

Also ever-present is the discordant refrain: 'But you'll never actually change anything.' This has been proven wrong many times over. Familiar, too, are the frustrating and frankly bizarre arguments made by governing élites against campaigns for the most basic human freedoms. So too the way that the law has consistently been used to repress radical activists and the way that the mainstream media has often cast them as subversive and dangerous criminals, even when they were advocating ideas that in years to come would be widely accepted as common sense.

There are plenty of other similarities – the blurry interplay between personalities and politics, the intrigues about who might be sleeping with whom and the ongoing tensions between established campaigning institutions and more radical grassroots networks. But most familiar of all is the passion, the energy and the sense of purpose awarded by a life committed to a cause, the oscillation between hope and despair, and the strength of relationships of the kind that can only be forged in struggle against adversity. This is the essence of campaigning, from the depths of history to the present day.

What struck me most was that the historical campaigns didn't only chime with contemporary movements but with one another too. All the successful campaigns appeared to have followed a fairly similar path, which I call in the book the stages of 'Consciousness', 'Co-ordination', 'Confrontation' and 'Consolidation'. They also seemed to resonate with the various theoretical works I studied – at least in part. The trouble was that most of the academic contributions viewed social change either from the perspective of the already powerful or from the supposedly objective sidelines. Only a few focused on the potential power of the have-nots. Nevertheless, even a cursory look at the past shows that the resistance of the oppressed is a major driver of history. That is what in this book is called Counterpower.

Counterpower is not a new term.[2] For example, in 1949 Martin Buber wrote that 'Power abdicates only under counter-power.'[3] In a 2003 edition of *New Internationalist*, social-movement theorist Graeme Chesters describes Counterpower as 'the shadow realm of alternatives, a hall of mirrors held up to the dominant logic of capitalism'.[4] In his book *Reflections on Empire*, Antonio Negri calls Counterpower 'an excessive overflowing force' and predicts that 'one day it will be unmeasurable'.[5] Yet he reflects that, beyond insurrection, the concept remains underdeveloped. But Counterpower means much more than insurrection and does not need to be violent to be effective. Indeed, in many cases armed 'revolutions' turn out not to be revolutions at all, but simply transitions of power from one élite to another.

This book seeks to develop the concept of Counterpower by looking at the different types of Counterpower people can use. The first is Idea Counterpower, which can be exercised by challenging accepted truths, refusing to obey and finding new channels of communication. The second is Economic Counterpower – exercised through strikes, boycotts, democratic regulation and ethical consumption. The third is Physical Counterpower – which can occasionally mean literally fighting back, or, alternatively, nonviolently placing our bodies in the way of injustice. Many of the most successful movements for transformational change have used all three kinds of Counterpower, while many of those that have fallen by the wayside have used only one or two.

One way of thinking about Counterpower is to use the analogy of political struggle taking place on a set of rudimentary scales, made of a plank of wood placed over a log, like a see-saw. On one side is the target and on the other is the movement. The target uses its economic power to pay or fire people; its idea power to use notions of natural authority to isolate campaigners; and its physical power to use security guards, police and military to intimidate, arrest or kill. The role of the movement is to exercise enough Counterpower to undermine these aspects of power and tip the balance in its favor. Again and again movements have shown that this can happen.

At first my research led to a sense of history repeating itself. But a closer reading revealed a steady evolution of strategy and tactics showing, for example, how the sophisticated methods of the Arab Spring are based on ideas that have been adapted and honed by revolutionaries across centuries. In preparation for the Egyptian Revolution, activists from the youth-led April 6 movement traveled to Serbia to learn from Srdga Popovic, who had been one of the leaders of the *Otpor* youth movement there which had been so successful in bringing down Slobodan Milosevic in 2000. Popovic was in turn heavily influenced by the work of Gene Sharp – a US scholar whose life has been dedicated to analyzing the methods of (amongst others) Lech Walesa, Martin Luther King Jr and Mohandas Gandhi.[6] One of the influences on Gandhi's outlook was the Russian Revolution of 1905 which was led by – amongst others – Leon Trotsky. Trotsky was of course a follower of Karl Marx, who was himself a keen student of the revolutions in France.[7] And so the lineage extends back through time.

The events of the Arab Spring are also giving renewed impetus to the social movements of today. Not long after Mubarak's resignation, Egyptian trade unions sent a solidarity delegation to the US, which was experiencing its most significant trade union movement struggle for a generation. In protest at repressive laws that would prevent public-sector workers from going on strike, thousands of activists occupied the Wisconsin Capitol building for 17 days, with hundreds sleeping there each night. Meanwhile, in Britain, protesters opposed to the restructuring of the welfare state along neoliberal lines adopted a new chant: 'London, Cairo, Wisconsin: We will fight and we will win'.

Only time will tell whether the Wisconsin protests were an important step towards something bigger or a brief peak of resistance. Similarly, whether the British anti-cuts movement will win its fight is so far unknown. So too the outcomes of events in North Africa and the Middle East. What is known, however, is that change *can* happen and *does* happen. But it rarely happens without Counterpower.

This book is written for anyone who is involved in movements for justice today – or who might be interested in becoming involved in the future. My aim is to get inside those campaigns of the past which are constantly referred to in the rhetoric of campaign rallies.[8] I hope to get to the root of *how* change happens, with the intention of providing a way for campaigners today to learn from the movements that constitute our heritage.

Friedrich Hegel is often credited with having said that 'The only thing we learn from history is that we don't learn from history'. It is up to us to prove him wrong.

1 6 Billion Ways, 5 March 2011, organized by Friends of the Earth, War on Want, Jubilee Debt Campaign, World Development Movement, City Circle and People & Planet. **2** See, for example, Ulrich Beck, *Power in the Global Age*, Polity, 2005, and Hisham Nazer, *Power of a Third Kind*, Praeger, 1999. **3** Martin Buber, *Paths in Utopia*, 1949, reprinted 1996 by Syracuse University Press. **4** *New Internationalist*, Sep 2003. **5** Antonio Negri, *Reflections on Empire*, Polity, 2008. **6** A journalist at the time of Serbia's 'Bulldozer Revolution' depicted Popovic 'scurrying around Belgrade with a heavily underlined copy of Sharp's tract stuffed in his pocket'. See Matthew Collins, *Time of the Rebels*, Serpents Tail, London, 2007. **7** Karl Marx, *The Eighteenth Brumaire of Louis Bonaparte*, 1852. Available at nin.tl/IQE8oi **8** In a speech for the TUC March for the Alternative demonstration in London on 28 March 2011, UK Labour Party leader Ed Miliband said: 'We come in the tradition of movements that have marched in peaceful but powerful protest for justice, fairness and political change. The suffragettes who fought for votes for women and won. The civil-rights movement in America that fought against racism and won. The anti-apartheid movement that fought the horror of that system and won.'

1

How Counterpower helps movements win

'*Freedom is never voluntarily given by the oppressor; it must be demanded by the oppressed.*'

Martin Luther King Jr

This book will make a bold claim: that a single idea helps explain why social movements past and present have succeeded, partially succeeded, or failed. Strategically applied, it has helped win campaigns, secure human rights, stop wars and even bring down governments. The name of the idea is rarely heard in public or academic parlance, but the idea is as old as history itself. It is called Counterpower.

When governments, corporations or other ruling institutions yield power, it is not through the goodness of their hearts. It is to save face when the people themselves have already claimed power. Of course, in theory, power can be voluntarily given away by those who already have it, but this has happened only rarely. Besides, what is given can more easily be taken back than that which is claimed. Overall, the lesson from our forebears is quite simple: for every aspect of power wielded by the 'haves', the 'have-nots' can wield yet more.

The classic definition of power – associated with the theorist Robert Dahl – is 'the ability for A to get B to do something that B would not otherwise have done'.[1] Counterpower turns traditional notions of power on their head. Counterpower is the ability of B to remove the power of A.

In the hands of the few, power can be called oppression, repression, exploitation or authoritarianism – the ability to do a lot at the expense of the many. Meanwhile, movements for freedom, emancipation, liberation, human rights and democracy have a common idea at their heart. That idea is Counterpower.

As this book will show, the Counterpower of the working class won the extension of the ballot and the Counterpower of disenfranchised women saw the introduction of universal adult suffrage.[2] The Counterpower of organized labor won rights in the workplace and the introduction of universal public services. The Counterpower of the Americans, the Irish, the Indians and the Africans, amongst others, won independence from colonial rule, and when the superpowers of West and East decided to reduce their funding of puppet regimes at the end of the Cold War, opposition movements used Counterpower to lead revolutions across the world.

Of course, it is a truism that no government past or present could survive if enough people organized effectively against it. After all, every government requires people to obey its orders. If enough people refuse to obey those orders, the government cannot govern. Therefore any campaign is winnable in theory. This raises two related questions. How can we win more campaigns? And why do we not win more often? These are the questions that this book will seek to answer, beginning by seeking to understand power itself.

The philosophical tradition of thinking about power 'from above' versus power 'from below' is well established. In Latin, *potentia* can be translated as 'power to', while *potestas* can be translated as 'power over'. 'Power from below' is implicit in the way we talk about campaigning. It is most plain to see (or hear) in hundreds of slogans: 'Black Power', 'Gay Power', 'Amandla!', 'The Workers United Will Never be Defeated', 'Whose Streets? Our Streets' and 'This Is What Democracy Looks Like' are only some of the examples. Quaker historians have described George Fox's struggle against religious persecution in the 17th century as 'speaking truth to power'. 'Power from below' is also a central theme of protest music, as in John Lennon's 'Power to the People', Patti Smith's 'People Have the Power', Billy Bragg's 'Power in a Union',[3] Public Enemy's 'Fight the Power' and 'Take the Power Back' by Rage Against the Machine.

It is because of the lack of a commonly used word in English that explicitly denotes 'power from below' that this book seeks to develop the term Counterpower. Power is when the few control the many; Counterpower is when the many resist the control of the few.

To the untrained eye, the power of élites is invisible, because we consider it normal. However it controls most people's lives.[4] Governments and other élites can make people do things by persuading them, paying them, or punishing them. Or we could say they have the power of the mind, money or muscle. The power of the mind can be used to influence how a person thinks, and therefore acts. The power of money can be used to pay someone to do something they would not otherwise do. And the power of muscle can be used to force someone into a particular course of action. I call these 'idea power', 'economic power' and 'physical power'.[5]

All of these types of power can be transformed into Counterpower through organization and resistance by ordinary people. We can mirror the power against us: we have access to what this book calls Idea Counterpower, Economic Counterpower and Physical Counterpower. If we can find ways to use these to undermine the power of the haves, then we are more powerful than they could possibly imagine.

This book is not only about the theory of change, although,

in the words of Judith Butler, 'theory is in itself transformative'.[6] The book is about celebrating and learning from the campaigns of others. To borrow a phrase from the author Milan Kundera, it is about 'the struggle of memory against forgetting'.[7] Let's begin by looking at how power and Counterpower have already been explained and used.

The power of ideas

History shows that whether we are talking about the divine right of kings, votes being reserved for the propertied classes, the supreme rule of the politburo or the 21st-century capitulation to the banks, those with power have always surrounded themselves with a cabal of sycophants, conservatives and beneficiaries, who have woven together a veil of philosophical legitimacy to win support for their dominance.

The philosopher Antonio Gramsci called this *hegemony* – that is to say, the control that élites can engineer through imposing and normalizing their view of the world. Gramscians call resistance to this 'counter hegemony', and resistance to dominant ideas 'ideological counter hegemony'. More simply, we can say that people are using Idea Counterpower – the practice of forming ideas that challenge the status quo and then communicating them.

The notion that the clash of arguments can lead to a greater truth is reflected in the theories and methods of philosophers reaching back to Socrates.[8] In what has since become known as 'dialectics', a dominant idea (a thesis) is challenged by another idea (an antithesis), leading to a compromise between the two – a synthesis, which becomes the new thesis. The promotion of an antithesis is what I call the use of Idea Counterpower. Despite the web of power conspiring to stop them, movements across the world have found innovative ways to make their voices heard.

Almost all movements have used the Idea Counterpower of public meetings, media engagement and persuasion. Some movements have gone further. At its best, Idea Counterpower is not only about informing people of events, but also about inspiring a change in worldview.

This has been a particular challenge for movements seeking to challenge the idea of Africans as subservient, second-class people. In the days of the struggle for the abolition of the slave trade, campaigners were faced with the task of persuading white populations that black people had equal rights. They did so with words, but when they did so with an image it was every bit as eloquent. The world-famous pottery designer Josiah Wedgwood produced a picture of a man on his knees, chains on his wrists and hands clenched in supplication. Underneath were written eight simple words: 'Am I not a man and a brother?'[9]

The design was used by US and British abolition societies, and was even printed on fashion items such as pipes and necklaces. It was part of the long struggle to change people's attitudes towards black people. Although the campaign against the transatlantic slave trade achieved its goal in the early 19th century, a wider struggle was necessary to challenge the ongoing view by many white people of black people as second-class citizens.

In 1957, as Ghana became the first African country to win black majority rule, a novel was published in Nigeria which helped to change attitudes amongst black and white people alike. *Things Fall Apart* by Chinua Achebe tells of the conflict between colonizers and colonized amongst the Igbo community of Nigeria, explains colonization from an African point of view and derides the colonialists' destruction of Igbo culture.[10] The very fact that a respected book which won global critical acclaim was written by an African gave inspiration to other Africans, and helped challenge the misconception held by many Europeans of Africa as a backward continent of savages.

As Nigeria's independence was later hijacked by military dictators, yet more Idea Counterpower was necessary. For decades, Nigeria's most popular musician Fela Kuti was a thorn in the side of successive authoritarian rulers. In audacious confrontation with the authorities, Fela's lyrics – penned in the Pidgin English of the masses – highlighted human rights abuses committed by corporations and governments in his country, and his music displayed an emotion and anger that words alone could not.[11]

Music can also be a powerful statement of identity and belonging, as reflected in the democracy campaigns of Estonia, Latvia and Lithuania in the late 1980s. These were named 'The Singing Revolutions' because of the role that mass singing of banned national songs had played in popular resistance. Notwithstanding these more philosophical roles of singing in protests, music can also make campaigning more enjoyable for people to *do*.

Another face of Idea Counterpower is to be found in Greenpeace co-founder Bob Hunter's concept of a 'media mind-bomb'. His vision was to produce media-friendly images, capable not only of drawing attention to certain issues and events, but of changing the consciousness of the world.

In his own words: 'The development of a planet-wide mass communications system... gives access to the collective mind of the species that now controls the planet's fate... If crazy stunts were required in order to draw the focus of the cameras that led back in to millions of brains, then crazy stunts were what we would do.'[12]

Greenpeace's first stunt was to try to sail a boat into the vicinity of a US nuclear weapons test off Amchitka. They never made it to the testing zone. But they achieved their objective of creating a media mind-bomb. News journalists reported their progress all the way. According to Hunter, 'as news manager for the expedition, I could censor any unflattering realities... I could arrange for events to be staged that could then be reported as news'. The testing was suspended a few months later.

It was a technique that the organization would use again and again – aided in 1977 by a grant from the World Wildlife Fund to purchase their own ship. A veritable wash of volunteers transformed it into an eye-catching charismatic vessel with an ear-catching name – the *Rainbow Warrior*. Over the ensuing years it chased whaling ships around the high seas. The strategy saw success when a commercial whaling moratorium was adopted by the International Whaling Commission in 1982.

Nick Gallie, a staff member at the time, explains why: 'A whaling ship, an explosive harpoon, a fleeing whale, and between them a tiny, manned inflatable with the word "Greenpeace" emblazoned on its side – it says it all. The image is a godsend for television news, and instantly hundreds of millions of people have shared an experience of Save the Whales. How many years of petitions and arguing over quotas in the International Whaling Commission could equal that?'[12]

However, the Counterpower of ideas is not restricted to conventional news engagement. Indeed, a host of obstacles have been placed in the way of movements through the ages, and still they have found ways to communicate their Idea Counterpower.

The concept of the media mind-bomb was reflected in the strategy of the youth-led democracy movement in Serbia in the early 2000s. Although they were very familiar with the possibilities for engagement with the global mass media, they themselves were under heavy restrictions. Nevertheless they thought up creative, media-friendly pranks to undermine the idea power of the regime of the dictator Slobodan Milosevic.

On one occasion, for example, activists placed a barrel on Belgrade's main shopping street with a picture of President Milosevic's face on it. Anyone was invited to bash it with a baseball bat. One activist remembers: 'In 15 minutes there were a hundred people in Knez Mihailova street beating the barrel... The police didn't know what to do... so they arrested the barrel! And they were photographed doing it and they were in the newspapers the next day. The whole country laughed.'[13]

An even more audacious prank came in the year 2000. Activists spoke loudly, on telephone lines they knew to be tapped, about a large delivery of campaign materials. Media were invited to observe the event. They watched as a van arrived and people started unloading boxes, staggering under their weight. The police moved in to impound the shipment but, to their surprise, the boxes were in fact very light indeed. They were completely empty. The country mocked the government once again.[14]

In other countries, both activists and the press are restricted by government. Under the military regime led by generals, including Than Shwe and Thein Sein, Burma has one of the most repressive anti-free speech regimes in the world. Expressing or distributing dissident views is punishable by imprisonment, torture or death. Doing so through the media is almost impossible, as every newspaper is first checked by state censors before publication. Yet still campaigners have found ways to get the word out.

In the summer of 2007, an advert appeared in the state-controlled broadsheet the *Myanmar Times*. It was supposedly from the Board of Islandic (sic) Travel Agencies 'Ewhsnahtrellik', saying that an old Danish poem describes the feeling in Burma: 'Feel Relaxed, Enjoy Everything, Dance on Minutes'. Logically read, the 'poem' was nonsense. However, if it is read laterally its message becomes clear – the stanza was in fact a mnemonic for FREEDOM. And the Scandinavian-sounding travel agency board? From back to front it read as 'Killer Than Shwe'.[15] The Burmese military ruler was being challenged in publications that his own regime had censored. This was one in a series of events that immediately preceded the Buddhist monks' peaceful uprising of August 2007, later dubbed 'the Saffron Revolution'. As these protests were repressed by police, campaigners attached pictures of Than Shwe to a number of stray dogs. To call someone a dog in Burma is a fiery insult. People saw these and smiled. Soldiers had to chase the dogs all day.[14]

So we can see that Idea Counterpower can mean much more than simply talking to people. Yet too often, campaigns use only the most pedestrian tactics. Even those that go beyond the conventional methods still often restrict themselves to Idea Counterpower alone. Idea Counterpower can on occasion help change minds. But if it fails, other forms of Counterpower are needed to force recalcitrant targets to change. One such option is Economic Counterpower.

The power of money

Economic power is derived from wealth, money, labor and land. It is most clearly seen in the ability to pay people to do things they would not otherwise do. Economic Counterpower is the refusal to work or the refusal to pay. The building of alternative economic power bases – such as trade unions, co-ops, progressive businesses, NGOs and publicly owned services – can also be seen as a form of Economic Counterpower.

The imbalance of power between employees and their managers was noted by Adam Smith. In *The Wealth of Nations* he writes: 'Masters are always and everywhere in a sort of tacit, but constant and uniform combination, not to raise the wages of labor above their actual rate. When workers combine, masters... never cease to call aloud for the assistance of the civil magistrate, and the rigorous execution of those laws which have been enacted with so much severity against the combination of servants, laborers and journeymen.'

Economic Counterpower is perhaps more poetically explained in the lyrics of numerous songs composed over the years. In 1915, a US trade unionist named Ralph Chaplain penned some lyrics which are still sung at many union gatherings today. To the tune of 'John Brown's Body':

> 'It is we who plowed the prairies; built the cities where they trade;
> Dug the mines and built the workshops, endless miles of
>   railroad laid;
> Now we stand outcast and starving midst the wonders
>   we have made;
> But the union makes us strong.'

The most obvious form of Economic Counterpower is the strike. A strike consists of a withdrawal of labor after negotiations over pay and conditions have broken down, or indeed in order to win recognition at all. Consider, for example, the case of the Justice for Janitors campaign in the US. Throughout the 1980s, wages and benefits for office cleaners in the US almost halved as companies outsourced their cleaning suppliers to agencies that undercut pay. In June 1990, a group of cleaners in Los Angeles decided that enough was enough and went on strike. Public support for the janitors surged when they attempted to march but were beaten back by police officers. Soon afterwards the union signed a contract for a wage increase of more than $2 per hour and the return of health benefits. This victory inspired cleaners across the country to organize for their rights too, precipitating the formation of the US-wide Justice for Janitors campaign.[16]

Sometimes strikes have more political ends. The general strike – the practice of a number of industries taking strike action at once – has proved an effective tactic for this. General strikes were instrumental in bringing about the establishment of the Soviet Union. They were also instrumental in resisting its control.

In 1980 Polish workers occupied their shipyard in Gdansk in protest at the firing of a popular colleague. Their act of resistance gave expression to widely held and deeply felt dissatisfaction with the regime. Within a day, solidarity strikes were taking place across the country. After a number of days, the Gdansk workers' initial demands were met, and some returned home. Some militants decided to stay, in solidarity with the other industries on strike. People from across the city flocked to the gates to show their support. The following day, many of the workers who had initially left returned to the shipyard. An inter-factory strike committee was formed, and agreed a bigger demand: the legal right to form independent trade unions. The deputy prime minister was dispatched to negotiate. At the insistence of the workers, the talks were broadcast live over the shipyard PA system and on television. The workers bided their time for two weeks. Eventually the economic pressure of so many industries on strike was too much. The government conceded the right to form independent trade unions in the country. The movement responded by doing so. They called their new union *Solidarność* (Solidarity).[17]

The following years saw martial law imposed, Solidarność outlawed, and then more strikes to legalize it again. In 1988 the trade union was invited to the negotiating table. This time it won not just independent trade unions, but democratic elections. In 1989, on the ninth anniversary of the beginning of the struggle, the Gdansk shipyard strike leader Lech Walesa was elected President of Poland.

The Soviet sphere of influence was further weakened by strikes in Africa. In the year of Walesa's election in Poland, a general strike was called in the West African state of Benin. It began when university students walked out, citing inadequacies in teaching and the payment of grants. They were soon joined by civil servants, plantation workers, medical workers, teachers and lecturers, few of whom had been paid. Because the leadership of the official trade unions was controlled by the government, new unofficial membership-led networks sprang up that united the protest movement further, and encouraged demands for civil and political rights to be made, alongside calls for economic and social rights. Soviet-backed President Mathieu Kerekou's initially repressive reaction emphasized the illegitimacy of the regime still more, exacerbated by stories of government corruption circulated by an increasingly confident press.

In February 1990, members of the ruling party, trade unionists, civil servants, embryonic political parties, former heads of state, religious leaders, agriculturalists and the military met for a nine-day meeting that would transform the future of the country, chaired by the country's Archbishop. On the third day, these delegates declared the conference sovereign, abolished the constitution and set in place procedures that would lead to elections. Benin's citizens went to the polls in November 1991, to vote in the first internationally recognized free and fair elections to be held in that country for 17 years.[18]

The campaign inspired a wave of revolutions across the continent. These rebellions took place not only against regimes that had been propped up by the Soviet Union, but also those supported by the West. In the following years there were regime transitions in more than half of the countries in sub-Saharan Africa.[19]

A rather smaller-scale version of a political strike is the Green Ban. The Green Ban is a commitment by a group of workers that they will not work on particular projects if they will be environmentally destructive or otherwise morally wrong. The term was coined in Australia in the 1970s when the New South Wales Builders Labourers' Federation in Sydney responded to the request of locals not to build on the only remaining bit of undeveloped bush land in the area. The developer was forced to abandon the project.[20]

In a variation on the Green Ban idea, the workforce of the British arms manufacturer Lucas Aerospace presented the company in 1976 with a plan to convert the factory from the manufacture of weapons to the production of more socially useful things. The plan was never put into practice, but it is an indicator of how far the idea of the Green Ban could go.

Refusing to work is just one form of Economic Counterpower. Refusing to pay is another. This can be represented in the form of a boycott – an effective tactic if enough people get behind it. One of the most famous boycotts in history is the Montgomery bus boycott. In the first half of the 20th century, segregation was an everyday reality for people in the southern United States. The segregation included the buses. Black people were required to stand if a white person wanted a seat, were not allowed to sit in reserved seats at the front of buses, and were not allowed even to sit next to a white person. In 1954, the Women's Political Council complained to the mayor, asking not for desegregation, but for fairer treatment. They were disregarded. However, an event the following year was enough to spark the touch paper.

On 1 December 1955, four black bus passengers were ordered to stand so that white passengers could sit. Three did so. One refused. Her name was Rosa Parks. When the Women's Political Council heard of this, they decided that the time was right for a bus boycott. When the day came, the buses were eerily quiet. African-Americans walked into town or traveled in taxis which agreed to charge only the bus fare rate. They also set up a new committee to oversee the campaign – the Montgomery Improvement Association. They elected as their chair someone who would become very famous indeed: Dr Martin Luther King Jr.

The boycott lasted more than a year. In the meantime the authorities refused to yield. They outlawed the taxi companies from offering solidarity fares. Martin Luther King and 100 others were charged with conspiracy. Extremists even bombed the houses of campaign leaders. But still the boycott held out. In the end the Economic Counterpower of the boycott merged with the Idea Counterpower it generated. On 13 November 1956, the Supreme Court ruled bus segregation unconstitutional. Not only did the movement succeed in desegregating the buses, it also helped launch the movement that would help deliver civil rights to black people across the United States.[21]

In recent times, the word 'boycott' has tended to be associated with the idea of a 'consumer boycott'. Yet the term originates from a refusal by Irish people in 1880 to pay rent to a hated British landlord – Captain Boycott – eventually causing him to leave the country. Notable examples of rent and tax boycotts can also be found in Scotland.

During the First World War, landlords in Glasgow decided to introduce massive rent increases in response to the influx of women moving to the city while their husbands were fighting in France. In response, the Glasgow Women's Housing Association was formed. Starting in the Govan area, they resolved to pay only their normal rent and not the increase. When the Govan women won their battle, they inspired others in the city to adopt similar methods. Eviction orders were served, but the women found creative ways of resisting the Sheriff's officers. They set up a number of sound signals to summon protesters at a moment's notice, and then squeezed into narrow passageways to blockade the bailiffs' path.

By October that year, 30,000 tenants were participating. In November, 18 non-payers were tried. Outside the courthouse, 10,000 people protested, threatening a general strike if the rents were not frozen. The government ordered the Sheriff to drop the charges. Shortly afterwards, the Rent Restriction Act was passed, fixing rents throughout the UK at their pre-war level for the duration of the First World War.[22]

The memory of the success of the Glasgow rent strike was far-reaching. Its spirit was evoked 72 years later in the very same city, with consequences that would once again benefit the entire country.

One of the key planks of Margaret Thatcher's 1987 election manifesto in the UK was the 'Community Charge' – a regressive, flat-rate local tax which would mean 'a cleaner living in a one bedroom flat would pay the same as the lord living in a castle.'[23] A contributor to the left-wing newspaper *Militant* calculated that the Thatcher family would save £2,300 (over $3,500) per year while an average family in Suffolk would pay an extra £640 (over $1,000).[24] It soon became known as the 'poll tax', a reference to an unpopular tax per head that had helped spark the Peasants' Revolt of 1381.

It was introduced in Scotland first, before being rolled out in England and Wales in 1990.[25] Following the 1987 general election, radicals in Scotland called on the Scottish Labour Party to support a non-payment campaign.[26] The support was not forthcoming.[27] The campaigners decided to fight on regardless. Anti-poll tax leagues emerged across Scotland, especially in Glasgow, with non-payment their preferred method. Thanks to public meetings, mass door-knocking campaigns and pledge-signing (all examples of Idea Counterpower), the support for the Economic Counterpower of non-payment became widespread. As the date for the extension of the poll tax to England and Wales approached, so the anti-poll tax organizations spread there too, using the same methods. In 1989 the All Britain Anti Poll Tax Federation was formed and elected the Glasgow activist Tommy Sheridan as its chair.[28] As local council after local council set their poll tax rates, mass protests took place on town hall steps right across the country. In Carlisle the council refused to implement the tax.

On 31 March 1990, the day before the introduction of the 'Community Charge' in England and Wales, 200,000 people marched through London, and a further 50,000 in Glasgow, with placards reading Pay NO Poll Tax. The anger soon erupted into violence, leading to mass riots in the streets of London. Despite the negative media coverage, opposition to the poll tax continued to rise.

Activists worked out that that if just 1 in every 37 people eligible to pay refused to do so the court system would be clogged up for 17 years. By mid-June, newspapers were reporting non-payment ratios of one in two in the larger cities. Campaigners found ways of elongating court procedure by representing themselves and making procedural points. On the first day that non-payers faced court, 1,800 summonses were thrown out. One campaigner said afterwards that 'I felt like we had scored at a Wembley Cup Final'.[29]

Activists also joined together in solidarity to resist bailiffs from entering houses. In Glasgow and London, tax collectors themselves protested at their orders to collect the unjust tax. In some areas the police declared that following up all of the defaulters would be physically impossible. However some were not so lucky. Amongst those imprisoned was the Labour MP Terry Fields, who spent 60 days in prison for refuing to pay his £373 (almost $600) poll tax bill.

As the Conservatives lost a string of by-elections, backbench MPs concluded that Margaret Thatcher had gone too far and that, were she to stay in office, their party would lose the next election. She was forced to stand down in November 1990, and the Conservatives chose a new leader. Under her successor the un-implementable poll tax plans were shelved indefinitely. In her autobiography, Thatcher complained that 'The eventual abandonment of the charge represented one of the greatest victories for these people ever conceded by a Conservative government.'[30]

In giving these examples of the effective use of both Idea Counterpower and Economic Counterpower, a third kind of Counterpower – that being used by the women and men who resisted the passage of bailiffs – has also been mentioned. This is Physical Counterpower.

The power of force

The 'right of revolution' is part of the philosophical foundations of the modern state. It is reflected in the United States Declaration of Independence and the French Declaration of the Rights of Man. The philosopher Jean-Jacques Rousseau (best known for his theory of the 'social contract') even advocated Citizens' Militias to keep the government in check.

The spirit was not confined to the 18th century. In 1961, Cuban revolutionary Che Guevara wrote: 'People must see clearly the futility of maintaining the fight for social goals within civil debate. When the forces of oppression come to maintain themselves in power against established law, peace is already considered broken.'[31] Although by no means a friend of Communist Cuba, US president John F Kennedy echoed Guevara's sentiment in a speech the following year in which he famously said: 'Those who make peaceful revolution impossible will make violent revolution inevitable.'[32]

Throughout history there have been uprisings against unjust rulers, many of them violent. Indeed, as far back as 2380 BCE, historians report a popular revolt in Sumer (part of modern-day Iraq) against the king. The French, American and English revolutions of the 17th and 18th centuries prepared the way for the parliaments of today. The 20th century bore witness to more than 200 armed uprisings, rebellions and revolutions across the world. Some got rid of colonizers, as in the case of the Irish War of Independence and Kenya's Mau Mau rebellion. Some replaced authoritarian feudalism with authoritarian communism – the Russian and Chinese revolutions being cases in point. Some brought down dictators – for example, the 1974 coup in Portugal and the long-running civil war in Ethiopia and Eritrea that eventually brought an end to the regime of Mengistu Haile Mariam in 1991. Others are commonly regarded as acts of terrorist violence which did not result in the overthrow of their enemies.

The power of revolutionary violence is perhaps best encapsulated by the most famous quotation of Mao Zedong: 'Political power grows out of the barrel of a gun.' This was not only how Mao seized power, but also how he maintained it. As we shall see in the third chapter, violence has been a strategy for responding to Counterpower movements by governments of left and right.

There are, however, alternative forms of Physical Counterpower that are nonviolent. Henry David Thoreau's 1849 essay *On Civil Disobedience* calls on readers not simply to wait for the next chance to vote for justice. That, he says, is as ineffective as wishing for justice. Instead, he advocates that people should actually be just, by which he meant refusing to co-operate with unjust laws or decrees. On the prospect of imprisonment (which he himself experienced) he declared: 'Under a government which imprisons any unjustly, the true place for a just man is also a prison.'

Some social movements have gone so far as to construct barricades and declare certain areas autonomous of government authority – the tented village in Egypt's Tahrir Square and (on a more modest scale) the climate camps in many Western countries are just two recent examples.[33] Such methods of refusing to be subject to the coercive power of the state are revolutionary. With some exceptions they are also usually temporary.

However, nonviolent Physical Counterpower is not only about refusing to co-operate, but also about actively getting in the way. This is what has become known as nonviolent direct action.[34] Although the term became popular in the latter part of the 20th century, the idea is much older. Indeed, one of the most celebrated and world-changing acts of resistance in history was an act of nonviolent direct action. It took place on 16 December 1773.

At that time, Britain imposed punitive import tariffs on tea to its American colony – with the result that its population was being taxed without their consent. For many years, activists used their Economic Counterpower of boycotts, arguing that they should not be forced to pay tax if they had no say in how it was spent.

In response to news that a large shipment of tea was headed to the colony from Britain, a mass meeting of activists was called to display the Idea Counterpower of reasoned argument and promote the Economic Counterpower of a boycott. However, for one group of activists, this wasn't enough. They left the public meeting early. Under the cover of nightfall they boarded three tea ships in Boston Harbor. Once on board, they managed to throw 342 chests of tea over the side in just three hours. This simple act of Physical Counterpower challenged Britain's economic power. It was backed up by Idea Counterpower, when the mainstream of the movement celebrated it as a legitimate act of resistance. It was one of the key events that led to the independence of the United States.[35]

Nonviolent direct action changed the US again in the 20th century. On 1 February 1960, four black students in North Carolina decided to disregard the unjust laws of segregation by the simple act of sitting at a whites-only lunch counter, politely ordering from the menu and waiting to be served. The service was refused, the students were asked to leave and the café closed early.

The next morning, the four returned, along with others. The following day, white students participated in the protests as well. On 5 February, 300 students arrived; on 6 February there were 1,400. The protests then spread to other lunch counters. By mid-February, there had been 54 sit-ins in 15 cities. In some places, racists responded by assaulting the demonstrators physically and verbally, as the police stood by and watched. The demonstrators responded with absolute nonviolence. By the end of February, the Physical Counterpower of the students started merging with Economic Counterpower as the eating places lost trade. It also merged with Idea Counterpower as people began to sympathize with the cause that the students had so successfully dramatized. In response, lunch counters changed their rules. The tactic had worked.[36]

Although condemned by some amongst the movement's older leadership, this method soon spread to other segregated institutions, such as libraries, art galleries and parks. The Idea Counterpower of publicity generated was a major factor in the passing of the Civil Rights Act of 1964, which mandated desegregation in US public institutions.

Many new methods of nonviolent direct action were developed during the early 1990s 'Roads Protests' in the UK. In 1989, the British government announced what it boasted would be 'The biggest road building program since the Romans'. Friends of the Earth challenged the decision through the established channels, including applying to the European Union and organizing small-scale protests. But when this route looked unlikely to succeed, the use of Physical Counterpower began. In February 1992, a group of travelers calling themselves the 'Dongas' decided to camp on the proposed site of the M3 motorway over Twyford Down. They were soon joined by members of the environmental group Earth First!, which had recently established itself in Britain.[37] Using tactics from the North American Earth First! manual they remained there for 10 months until security guards were employed to clear the site.

One participant called Twyford 'an absolutely successful campaign in every respect except stopping the road'.[38] It did, however, reap rewards. When a similar alliance of groups began making preparations for a campaign at another site, Oxleas Wood near Greenwich, the government announced that the project would not be going ahead.

Boosted by the victory, campaigners began to organize against plans for the extension of the M11 in Essex. This time the campaign was less about protecting an area of natural beauty and more about protecting a community, as the road was going to cause the demolition of a number of houses. Organizers engineered a number of media-friendly confrontations to highlight their cause – the first being the defense of an ancient tree on Wanstead Common. First schoolchildren, then parents, then other local residents joined in, helping to provide a base of activists to sustain direct action for the next year.

As they occupied the proposed construction site, the police employed professional climbers to evict them. Other parts of the climbing community saw this as a sell-out and lent their skills to the protesters. People hung themselves in netting, built tree-houses and learned how to climb on to roofs. People locked themselves into holes in the road, sealed themselves in basements of houses and even built a tunnel which allowed people to re-enter the site once they had been evicted. Police prepared for months to clear the site. When they finally came to do so it took them days on end. Eventually only a scaffolding tower remained – covered with grease. The sole activist at the top extended the occupation by a further day. The overall operation cost the police millions, a not insignificant amount of which was due to the single activist in the tower. The campaign was covered by media across the world.

These tactics were developed still further in the campaign against the Newbury Bypass in 1996. Entire 'sky villages' were constructed above while underground tunnels were dug below. This time, the activists also took steps to hamper the efforts of the security guards to remove them. For example, they blockaded the security access road with a giant tripod – a set of three poles with an activist sitting at the top. Once again, the press followed every move and made something of an accidental celebrity of one eco-warrior who used the pseudonym 'Swampy'.

The local Friends of the Earth group had been involved in the Newbury campaign long before the arrival of the tree-sitters. The campaign opened up Friends of the Earth to a wider variety of tactics as it worked with different groups of campaigners, supplied legal observers and organized a mass rally near the site. The campaign gave focus and impetus to the lobbying in London.

All three projects went ahead, but the campaign had a wider effect. As protests continued in Glasgow, Bath, Newcastle and elsewhere, the Physical Counterpower of the protesters created a serious economic headache for the government. The public attention attracted by the audacious acts of civil disobedience also contributed to the growth of Idea Counterpower on this issue. The reports and lobbying of NGOs were given greater attention, as were the local grassroots residents' groups. The roads project became more and more unpopular. In 1996, the British government decided to abandon its road-building strategy, cut billions from the roads budget and axe plans for 77 new roads. The protesters' efforts had paid off.

Using Counterpower

The stories above have exemplified different kinds of Counterpower. But some of them used all three. The central tactic of the Glasgow rent strikers and the poll tax non-payment campaign was Economic Counterpower – but this was only effective alongside the Idea Counterpower of building public support and the Physical Counterpower to repel bailiffs. The media mind-bombs of Greenpeace are undoubtedly a form of Idea Counterpower, but they are based on the Physical Counterpower of getting in the way and the Economic Counterpower of raising independent funds for the organization. Some, like the roads protests, only used two kinds of Counterpower. Yet through them they identified the sources of governmental power and found ways to undermine it.

It should be noted, too, that while the examples given here have been about large-scale change, these principles apply every bit as much to smaller-scale struggles. Take a case I recently read about, involving a temping agency which reportedly assured an employee that he wouldn't need to fill in a timesheet for a small number of days worked, then proceeded to refuse to pay him for them. In response, people picketed the agency and contacted people in other cities to encourage them to do likewise at other branches. Although an escalation strategy was planned, in the end little more than Idea Counterpower was needed to make the company back down. However, by threatening the agency's source of power – namely money from new clients – the group won and the employee was paid what he was owed.

There is a case to be made that Counterpower is not only a tactic but a good unto itself. If groups can provide accountability from below, élites of whatever kind will be less likely to be able to exploit them. This is most clearly to be seen by looking at unionized workplaces where, on average, wages are higher, conditions are better and workers are more likely to be consulted on major decisions. This transfers to community campaigning too. Although local officials frequently face pressure from above to change things in certain ways, there are countless examples of community groups utilizing Counterpower to counterbalance that pressure and win positive change in their localities. Indeed, it is likely that even if headline campaigns are lost, the very presence of a group with the ability to make life difficult for the powerful makes it harder for them to ignore local opinion.

In the light of such examples, it may seem obvious that social movements using Counterpower have more chance of success. But this idea is not universally held. One alternative approach frequently proposed is *power over* – for example by winning elections or seizing state power in other ways. But, as this book will show, radical politicians tend to be elected only after having been part of mass movements. Even once elected, they are more likely to stick to their principles if the extra-parliamentary movement uses Counterpower to ensure that they do so.[40]

Another version of *power over* is to make backroom deals with the powerful. Again it is true that speaking to those in power can be a useful thing for campaigners to do. But it is severely limited without Counterpower. No matter who negotiators are talking to, a 'bargaining chip' is needed. That can only be achieved through Counterpower. Without it, the change that can be won is at best microscopic – and could be counterproductive if it serves to lend legitimacy to the very power structures that the movement is challenging. At worst, it leads to a small minority of the movement gaining disproportionate power and becoming a mouthpiece for the system that they initially sought to change. Some movements specifically guard against this possibility by refusing to allow individuals to speak on their behalf. Targets are then left with only two options: submit to a critical mass of demands or devote substantial resources to repressing the opposition.

Another alternative strategy to Counterpower is *antipower*. Its advocates often repeat the famous (mis)quote 'Power corrupts, absolute power corrupts absolutely'.[41] In contrast, Counterpower strategies are in line with the words of Martin Luther King Jr, who wrote: 'There is nothing essentially wrong with power. The problem is that in America power is unevenly distributed.'[42]

Power today is unevenly distributed on a global scale. Yet some associated with modern social movements insist that personal salvation alone can lead to widespread change. Personal morality and collective consciousness are both helpful, even necessary, for social change. But they are not of themselves strategies. King too argued along these lines: 'The concepts of love and power are usually contrasted as polar opposites. Love is identified with a resignation of power and power with a denial of love. What is needed is a realization that power without love is reckless and abusive, and love without power is sentimental and anemic. Power at its best is love implementing the demands of justice.'[42]

The final and most common alternative to Counterpower is simply to accept power as it is. This is based on the assumption that if only we design good ideas and communicate them to those in power they will take notice. But policy-making is not a process of finding the best solution for the most people. Government policy is a reflection of the balance of power in society. Even if a civil servant presents an objective set of policy options to a minister, the politician responsible must then ask herself, 'will I keep my job if I allow this to happen?'

Some social-movement strategists do, however, understand the role of Counterpower. For example, Michael Albert argues that movement victories are achieved by 'raising unendurable social costs to élites', which he defines as 'costs embodied in the threat that the conditions of their privilege will unravel if their policies don't succumb to pressure'.[43]

Although these words were written in 2001, similar sentiments can be seen in a philosophy far older. Indeed, they are reflected in the life and work of a man who started a process which transformed the map of the world. His name was Mohandas Gandhi. It is to the development of his ideas from theory to practice that the next chapter will look.

1 Andrew Heywood, *Politics,* Palgrave, London, 2002. **2** Although some prisoners and some mental health patients are still awaiting the right to vote. **3** This is also the title of a different song by IWW (Industrial Workers of the World) member Joe Hill in the 1910s. **4** This links to Steven Lukes' 'Third Face of Power' see Mark Haugaard (ed), *Power: A Reader*, Manchester University Press, 2002. **5** This corresponds with Michael Mann's classifications: economic power, ideological power, military power and political power – see Haugaard, op cit. It also reflects JK Galbraith's classifications of Condign Power, Compensatory Power and Conditioned Power which he explained in *The Anatomy of Power*, Houghton Mifflin, Boston, 1983. **6** Judith Butler, *Undoing Gender*, Routledge, London, 2004. **7** Milan Kundera, *The Unbearable Lightness of Being*, Faber & Faber, London, 1984. **8** Dialectical thought is particularly associated with Hegel and Marx. **9** Mike Ashley, *Taking Liberties: The Struggle for Britain's Freedoms and Liberties*, British Library, 2008. **10** Chinua Achebe, *Things Fall Apart*, Penguin, London, 1957. **11** Read Carlos Moore, *Fela: This Bitch of a Life*, Alison and Busby, London, 2010, for an account of his life, or search for 'Zombie' to listen to one of his most famous and most provocative songs. **12** Fred Pearce, *Green Warriors: The People and the Politics behind the Environmental Revolution*, Bodley Head, London, 1991. **13** Srdja Popovic interviewed in Matthew Collin, *The Time of the Rebels: Youth Resistance Movements and 21st Century Revolutions*, Serpent's Tail, London, 2007. **14** See Steve Crawshaw and John Jackson, *Small Acts of Resistance: How Courage, Tenacity and Ingenuity can Change the World*, Union Square, New York, 2010. **15** Cutting from *Myanmar Times*, Aug 2007. **16** See nin.tl/mAjn7N **17** See Peter Ackerman and Jack DuVall, *A Force More Powerful: A Century of Nonviolent Conflict*, St Martin's, New

York, 2000. **18** J Heilbrunn, 'The Social Origins of National Conferences in Benin and Togo', *Journal of Modern African Studies*, Vol 31, No 2, 1993. **19** Michael Bratton, and Nicholas Van de Walle, *Democratic Experiments in Africa: Regime Transitions in Comparative Perspective*, Cambridge University Press, 1997. **20** See Verity Burgman and Meredith Burgman, *Green Bans, Red Union*, UNSW, 1998. **21** See Gene Sharp, *Waging Nonviolent Struggle*, Porter Sargeant, Boston, 2005. **22** See nin.tl/l4i9Nw **23** Glyn Harries, *Hackney Heckler*, May 2011 or for a fuller account including images read Danny Burns, *Poll Tax Rebellion*, AK Press, Stirling, 1992. **24** Quoted in Peter Taafe, *The Rise of Militant*, 1995, available online at socialistparty.org.uk/militant **25** Despite the lack of support for the Conservative Party in Scotland. **26** From the Militant Tendency grouping which at that point was part of the Labour Party but was subsequently purged. **27** A proposal to oppose 'illegality' was supported by 2-1 at the Scottish Labour Party congress. **28** Sheridan was elected to the Scottish Parliament in 1999. **29** Taafe, op cit. **30** Margaret Thatcher, *The Downing Street Years*, quoted in Taafe, op cit. **31** Che Guevara, *Guerrilla Warfare*, Monthly Review Press, New York, 1961. **32** Speech to Latin American Diplomatic Corps. **33** Other examples include the Chiapas communities in Mexico, the Heroic Vietnam Quarter in Paris, the roads protest sites, the self-governing townships in South Africa. **34** Often referred to as NVDA. **35** Allison Stark Draper, *The Boston Tea Party*, Rosen, New York, 2000. The exact sequence of events is disputed by historians. **36** nin.tl/lWOzm6 **37** At this point Friends of the Earth left the campaign, worried about the possible PR implications of being seen to work with Earth First. However, seeing the success of the Twyford campaign, tentative relationships were rebuilt for other protests. **38** Roger Geffen, April 2011. **39** *Freedom*, Vol 72, No 10, 21 May 2011. **40** Cross-country studies of environmental campaigning show that there is most progress where green campaigners enter government *and* the movement continues in oppositional campaigning to persuade them to put their principles into practice, see John Dryzek, Christian Hunold, David Schlosberg, David Downes and Hans-Christian Hernes, 'The Environmental Transformation of the State: the USA, Norway, Germany and the UK', *Political Studies*, Vol 50, 2002. **41** The full quotation is usually stated as 'Power tends to corrupt and absolute power corrupts absolutely. Great men are almost always bad men, even when they exercise influence and not authority.' **42** Martin Luther King, *The Autobiography of Martin Luther King Jr*, Abacus, New York, 1999. **43** Michael Albert, *Who Owns the Movement?*, ZNet, Nov 2001.

2
How India won its independence

'A nonviolent revolution is not a program of seizure of power. It is a program of transformation of relationships ending in peaceful transfer of power.'

Mohandas Gandhi

History provides numerous examples of revolutions that have taken place without civil wars or coups. A program of strikes, civil disobedience and demonstrations led to the end of colonial rule in Ghana in 1957. This set off what Harold Macmillan called the 'Wind of Change' which swept colonists from power in dozens of African countries. In the late 1980s, there were nonviolent revolutions in Poland, Czechoslovakia, Estonia, Latvia and Lithuania. Concurrently, the nonviolent revolution in Benin precipitated a second wave of democratic transitions in Africa. In the early 2000s, Serbia's largely nonviolent 'Bulldozer revolution' became the first of what became known as the 'Color Revolutions', including Georgia's 'Rose Revolution' of 2003, and Ukraine's 'Orange Revolution' of 2004. During the 'Arab Spring' of 2011, largely unarmed revolutions in Tunisia and Egypt dislodged the unelected rulers of those countries.

Although he didn't live to see them, every one of these campaigns was informed to some extent by the philosophy of Mohandas Gandhi, who led the nonviolent movement against colonial rule in India. Gandhi explained his version of Counterpower using language linked to the Hindu religion with which many of his audience of the day would identify. He named his preferred method of civilly disobedient resistance *Satyagraha*. The word is made up of the Sanskrit words *satya* ('truth') and *agraha* ('holding firmly to'), which could also be translated as 'truth force' or even 'love force'.

Satyagraha is a form of Idea Counterpower which recognizes that the law itself is a social construct – a form of idea power. Therefore non-adherence to the law undermines this aspect of the power wielded by governments. However, as we will see, the method also encompasses Economic and even Physical Counterpower, providing that it is nonviolent.

Gandhi could see some practical evidence that his theories were correct by looking at the events of 1905 in Tsarist Russia. There, the popular and largely peaceful general strike of 1905 led to Tsar Nicolas II promising reforms including freedom of speech, freedom of association, an end to imprisonment without trial and even an elected parliament – the (short-lived) Duma. Gandhi concluded that 'Even the most powerful cannot rule without the co-operation of the ruled'.[1]

Gandhi was not only a follower of international affairs, but also a keen student of philosophy. During his periodic stays in prison he made his own self-education a priority. Three writers had a particularly strong influence on this thinking. First was John Ruskin. In his book *Unto This Last* (which Gandhi translated into Gujarati), Ruskin advocated simplicity, equality and community. This was a great influence on Gandhi's decision to set up ashrams in South Africa and India based on such principles. Second was

Leo Tolstoy, who in *The Kingdom of God is within You* presents violence as incompatible with Christianity and recounts stories of Quakers putting nonviolent resistance into action. In 'Letter to a Hindu' – an essay on India's freedom struggle which Gandhi reprinted in his newspaper – Tolstoy suggests that protests and strikes can be seen as the application of love. These ideas were brought together in Gandhi's mind with his Hindu religion, aided by his lifelong friendship with the third writer – Shrimad Rajchandra, a Jain poet and philosopher. All of these ideas are reflected in Gandhi's philosophy of Satyagraha.

Gandhi developed his theory of change during his time working with the Indian community's struggle for civil rights in South Africa. When he used the principles of *Satyagraha* to win a campaign against a cap being put on Indian immigration, he began to show how nonviolent uses of Counterpower could work in practice. Over the following decades, he would use these tactics to help liberate India, the country of his birth, from imperial rule.

The colonization of India

India was amongst the many regions, countries and peoples across the world that were colonized through a combination of economic, physical and idea power. The East India Company was set up on 24 September 1599.[2] It was in many ways a precursor to the transnational corporations of today. Its 125 shareholders had one interest: profit – especially given the significant upfront capital cost of £72,000. Queen Elizabeth I granted the company exclusive trading rights with India and soon ships were regularly dispatched to India's shores, returning with spices, sugar, raw silk and cotton. The relationship was not mutually beneficial – or rather it was not beneficial for the majority of Indians. It suited a few local rulers, from whom the company bought favor through privileged access to material rewards. The practice continued for more than two and a half centuries.

A Company official wrote in 1817 that: 'Our inexperience and our ignorance of the circumstances of the people make it more necessary for us to seek the aid of regular establishments to direct the internal affairs of the country, and our security requires that we should have a body of head men of villages interested in supporting our dominion.'[3] But where economic power was not sufficient, the East India Company had no qualms in using physical force to get its way. The Company commanded a large army, which it used to wrest power from local rulers who did not co-operate on its terms.

In 1857, Indian soldiers working for the Company began to mutiny – initially in response to the racism of their bosses, and then against the British presence in India itself. The rebels took control of several towns and expelled British soldiers. Reinforcements were sent from Britain, whose organization and weapons eventually overpowered the Indian rebels. Nevertheless, the Indian Mutiny (later referred to as 'The First War of Indian Independence') displayed enough Physical Counterpower to begin the process that led to the once-mighty East India Company being forced to dissolve. But there was not enough Idea Counterpower to communicate a coherent way forward for the country, nor enough Physical Counterpower to win the war. Administration of the country was handed over to the British Government. And so, in 1858, Britain's direct rule of India began.

Like the East India Company before them, the new colonizers were adept at using the divisions between different ethnic and religious groups to prop up their own power and thus enable them to rule the country. After physical power won control of the country, the new rulers used economic power to maintain it. The new governors paid Indians to staff a civil service and police force that would administer and enforce the colonizers' laws. In such a way, a new layer of Indian society was established whose economic interests became allied with the maintenance of the British Empire.

This time, the domination was accompanied by propaganda that associated control of India with emotions such as British pride and patriotism. This is reflected in a later quotation from Rudyard Kipling, who declared: 'The responsibility for governing India has been placed by the inscrutable design of providence upon the shoulders of the British race.'[4] Such was the multifaceted power structure that independence activists faced. It took almost 100 years, but eventually they overcame it.

The Indian National Congress

The Indian National Union was formed on the initiative of a British civil servant in 1885 as a forum for educated élites to converse with the authorities, thus embedding the legitimacy of colonial rule. Their first 'campaign' involved asking the voters of Britain to elect representatives who might be sympathetic to the INU's concerns. It had very little impact. Later that year they changed their name to the Indian National Congress.

In the early days the Congress was just that – an annual gathering with discussions, speeches and resolutions. Over time, elements emerged that argued for the use of Counterpower. For example, in 1902, Bal Gangadhar Tilak appealed: 'Though downtrodden and neglected, you must be conscious of your power of making the administration impossible if you choose to make it so.'[1] At the time, Tilak was considered an extremist. Yet within 13 years this idea was to form the basis of Indian National Congress strategy.

Some independence leaders, Gandhi included, supported Britain during World War One, in the hope that this might lead to a more sympathetic hearing for the case for decolonization. But they were wrong. Britain thanked the Indian independence movement for its support by introducing the Rowlatt Act – legislation to restrict 'seditious acts' and anti-government activity. It extended the period during which those involved in revolutionary activities could be imprisoned without trial to two years.

It fell upon the Indian National Congress to construct a response. Some so-called 'moderate' politicians suggested that merely accepting the changes might be the most effective tactic. Yet after such an approach having so demonstrably failed in the recent past, such views were in something of a minority. The use of Physical Counterpower through armed uprising was morally opposed by Gandhi, and his colleagues agreed that, whether morally right or wrong, it was tactically unlikely to be successful – especially given the nature of the Act. The path of nonviolent Physical Counterpower was also difficult because, as the Act would not affect the majority of Indians, it could not easily be directly disobeyed on a wide scale.

That left the possibilities of Economic Counterpower and Idea Counterpower at the movement's disposal. These were the routes that they took. A nationwide day of prayer, fasting and refusal to work was called for 7 April 1919. The call also included a suggestion to read banned literature – including Gandhi's book *Hind Swaraj* ('Indian Home Rule'). Through the simple act of closing their shops and leaving their classrooms, thousands were able to show their solidarity and use their Economic Counterpower. By reading books and visiting the temple, they could also demonstrate their Idea Counterpower.

The authorities were worried, and prevented Gandhi from traveling where he had intended. As rumors spread of his arrest, protests turned violent. Gandhi was disappointed and called for the end of civil disobedience. The authorities turned fire on the campaign – metaphorically by banning all public meetings and then, when this order was disobeyed, literally.

On 13 April, thousands of people illegally but peacefully gathered in Jallianwala Bagh – a garden in the city of Amritsar. They took it in turns to speak out, defying the restrictions placed upon their city. After almost an hour of speeches and applause, 50 imperial soldiers filed into the closed space. Without warning, they opened fire. The Indian National Congress estimated that 1,500 people died. Soon afterwards, resistance leaders across the country were imprisoned and tortured.

The government's show of physical power caused untold suffering. Conversely, it also boosted the movement, making the importance of resistance clear to many. The Indian National

Congress responded by dropping its membership fees and for the first time seriously recruiting to become a mass political party. Gandhi toured the country giving speeches. Amongst the resistance tactics he advocated was a boycott of British-made cloth. In the cities, great fires were made of imported cloth and rough homespun garments soon became the uniform of the movement. The simple Indian spinning wheel became the independence movement's symbol.

Gandhi's speeches from this time contain a brilliant evocation of the concepts at the heart of Counterpower: 'The British want us to put our struggle on the plane of machine guns where they have the weapons and we do not,' he said. 'Our only assurance of beating them is putting the struggle on a plane where we have the weapons and they do not.'[1] This time of building helped prepare the movement for the most intense period of civil disobedience, which came eight years later, in 1930.

The Salt March

Like the first wave of resistance, the second major campaign was also triggered by the British. This time they set up a commission to investigate their governance arrangements for India. However, not a single Indian was included on it. The message was clear: Britain did not think that Indians should have a say in deciding their own future. It was instead constituted of seven British MPs. No-one could have known it at the time, but one of the commission's number would later become Britain's Prime Minister – Clement Attlee.

The Indian National Congress and the Muslim League opted to boycott the commission. Everywhere the commission members went, they were met by protesters brandishing black flags. The views of the population could not have been in doubt to the visitors. As an alternative to the British commission,[5] the independence movement adopted 'the Nehru Report', calling for dominion status within the British Empire. In a compromise between moderates and militants (the latter demanded full independence), Congress offered the British government until the end of 1929 to accept the moderate report. Otherwise a nonviolent struggle for full independence would be launched. The British rejected the offer.

After a period of reflection, Gandhi advised the Indian National Congress to begin by focusing their nonviolent campaign upon a commodity of equal importance to Hindus and Muslims, an injustice that disproportionately hurt the poorest, and a food that, ironically, he had forsaken some years previously: salt. Despite the fact that salt lay in abundance along the coast, the authorities claimed an exclusive monopoly on its manufacture and sale. The establishment seemed untroubled by Gandhi's plan. British Viceroy Lord Irwin wrote in a letter to his homeland that 'At present the prospect of a salt campaign does not keep me awake at night',[1] while *The Statesman* newspaper scoffed: 'It is difficult not to laugh, and we imagine that will be the mood of most thinking Indians'.[6] But they were wrong to dismiss the plan so soon.

Gandhi's plan mobilized not just Idea Counterpower but Economic Counterpower too. He resolved to walk 240 miles (384 kilometers) to the sea, before leading a countrywide move to make and sell salt. The journey began on 12 March, at 6.30am, in Gandhi's home town. At every village along the way Gandhi was met by supportive people making noise. With each speech, Gandhi implored village officers to resign, and promoted social boycotts against those who refused – leading almost a third of officials in the Surat region to resign during that time. He also spoke of the impending campaign of targeted lawbreaking. The spectacle of the small, educated man dressed in little but a loincloth leading such a pilgrimage captured worldwide attention. National newspapers and newsreels from across the world reported the progress of the march. As knowledge of the movement spread, ever greater numbers joined: 30,000 at Surat and then 50,000 at the railhead for Dandi.

As the sun rose on 6 April, Gandhi and his followers

marched on to the beach. With more than a hint of drama, Gandhi reached down to pick up a clump of salty mud and raised it in the air. This was the signal for the campaign of civil disobedience to begin. There and then marchers began to make their own salt from sea water – in direct contravention of the law of the land. The movement's leaders played a full part in the non-cooperation, selling illegal salt themselves on the streets of India's biggest cities, often surrounded by rings of people with arms linked together to keep the police at bay.

Up and down the country people followed this example by openly making their own salt. The authorities were caught in a trap. To allow the illegality to go ahead would show weakness, while to prevent it by physical force would be to make martyrs of the movement's leaders. British Secretary of State for India William Wedgwood Benn (father of leftwing politician Tony Benn) understood Gandhi's strategy perfectly, observing: 'They are deliberately attempting to present us with the alternative of using what they will represent to be unjustifiable and tyrannical repression or conceding to their demands'.[1]

With the resistance widespread, Gandhi organized a visual focus for the confrontation. He announced that he would lead a nonviolent raid on the Dharasana salt works, thus proposing to use the movement's Physical Counterpower to challenge the economic power of the occupiers. Gandhi was arrested on the eve of the planned action. But this expected setback did not stop it from going ahead. Over a period of three weeks, protesters walked to the fence of the salt works every day and attempted to pull it down. Each time they were met with brutal force and struck down by police. Stretchers carried off the wounded.

The confrontations were not, however, confined to Dharasana. In the city of Lucknow, local organizers called for demonstrations in the British areas of town. They refused to apply for salt-making licenses because to do so would be to recognize the authority of the British Raj. They too were met with violent force. Public assemblies and demonstrations were banned and a curfew was installed.

The government crackdown was widespread. The authorities called for the arrest of anyone involved in 'no tax' protests, and other leaders of the Indian National Congress were sent to prison, where Gandhi remained. Each effort to crush the movement was reported in the newspapers and won new supporters. In response to the government restricting the flow of communication from the Indian National Congress to local communities, people found their own ways to resist and their own local organizers to co-ordinate it. The 'set-piece' confrontations subsided, to be replaced by local community-based resistance.

In Gujarat, campaigners withheld rent from their British landlords in protest at Gandhi's imprisonment. After some months, the authorities responded by sending police officers *en masse* to attack locals, tie them up and strip them of their valuables. In Uttar Pradesh, the authorities threatened to destroy campaigners' crops. Some tribal peoples used civil disobedience to address a long-held grievance – lack of access to forests. Disregarding government warnings, large numbers entered the forests to cut wood and graze livestock. Resistance in other parts of India was focused on the *chaukidaris* – Indian officials paid to report local goings-on to the imperial police. Chaukidaris faced social boycotts and villagers refused to pay those taxes that funded the chaukidaris' salaries. The confrontation continued in the cities as well. On 12 December, for example, a group tried to prevent trucks carrying foreign goods into Bombay by lying in the road in front of them. One young activist was killed, prompting mass demonstrations that were met by armed police.

A total of 60,000 people were imprisoned for their role in the civil disobedience campaign. This cost the government a huge amount of money – in addition to the costs of policing the frequent demonstrations. At the same time, tax receipts on salt and cloth were falling. By this point the drop in the value of cloth was particularly dramatic – it fell by 50 per cent over a 12-month period.[1] Most worryingly for the British Raj, its physical power was also under challenge. The Indian police tasked with dispersing demonstrations were subject to intense social boycotts, often being refused service in shops and being shouted at in the street. The British began to worry whether it would be possible to maintain their loyalty under such conditions.

Yet compromises in the Indian independence movement meant that its Counterpower did not reach its full potential. In order to keep Indian business owners on side, no strike action was called – for that could have hurt Indian as well as British business. The choice of Hindu imagery also meant that the Idea Counterpower was presented in a way that was less likely to appeal to Muslims. As a result, Hindus and Muslims did not participate equally.

The imperial government won the battle. It gained the upper hand as land seizures, imprisonments and beatings took their toll. In the end, Gandhi was forced to accept a truce. The concessions he negotiated are testament to the effectiveness of the Counterpower the movement had utilized. The government agreed to release nonviolent prisoners, to unban proscribed organizations and to allow salt to be made in coastal areas. But these concessions came at a price. India was not granted self-rule at that time, and the civil-disobedience campaign was called off. Gandhi traveled to London to join another roundtable conference on self-rule, but it came to nothing. Or so he thought.

Meanwhile in Britain...

Gandhi was regarded with suspicion by many within the British establishment. Most notably, Winston Churchill called Gandhi a 'half-naked fakir' and expressed outrage at the fact that such a man was negotiating 'on equal terms with the representative of the king-emperor'. However, it was not a view shared by all British people. On his visit to the country in 1930-1, Gandhi was welcomed with open arms by many factory workers, even those whose products he had been boycotting. The Idea Counterpower of the independence movement had long been rippling far beyond India's shores.

One of the most prominent British advocates of Indian independence was Annie Besant. As part of a life which also included supporting the Matchgirls' Strike (a celebrated example of Counterpower from London's East End in 1888), campaigning for free school meals and advocating birth control, she served a term as the first female President of the Indian National Congress in 1917.[7] As a journalist, activist and orator, her work not only helped co-ordinate the struggle in India, but also maintained the interest of her contacts in Britain. In her autobiography she writes: 'I lifted up my voice in all our great towns, trying to touch the consciences of the people, and to make them feel the immorality of a land-stealing, piratical policy... I was denounced as an agitator, a firebrand.'[8]

Indian self-rule was also an issue of concern to Keir Hardie – the self-educated Scottish miner who became Britain's first independent socialist MP before co-founding the Independent Labour Party, then the Labour Representation Committee and eventually the Labour Party, of which he was the first leader. He too visited India to meet with independence campaigners and pledge his support.

In 1924, Ramsay MacDonald – known personally to both Besant and Hardie – became prime minister as leader of a minority Labour government. Before his election he had given a number of speeches in favor of Indian self-determination. However, he toned down his previous sentiment to gain the support of Liberal MPs for his premiership. A leftwing newspaper of the time opined that 'The attitude of the Labour Government has indirectly helped the cause of Indian freedom, while it has damned the Labour aristocracy'.[9]

By 1931 MacDonald (who chaired the roundtable talks) was maintaining office without the support of the Labour Party and was relying on the votes of the Conservatives and Liberals instead. The parliamentary arithmetic was hardly favorable to the Indian cause but a bill was eventually signed in 1935 that extended the franchise to millions more Indians and for the first time allowed Indian majorities to form local governments with limited powers. Just four years later, Britain showed how limited those powers were.

The Second World War

In September 1939, Viceroy Linlithgow announced that India would be fighting in the Second World War on the side of Britain. His announcement came as news to Indians themselves. None of the structures established in the 1935 reforms were consulted. Congress members responded by standing down from their seats.

In many ways the independence movement was in a stronger position than ever before. The Second World War meant that Britain's power in India was considerably weakened as its economic and military resources were transferred to the war effort. As hundreds of thousands of Indians risked their lives as soldiers, Britain became more reliant on Indian obedience than ever before. However, many Indians did not want to obey.

Fearing a rebellion, and seeking the support of the Indian National Congress for the war effort, leftwing cabinet minister Stafford Cripps was dispatched to negotiate. But he was unable to offer either immediate self-government or an agreed timeframe for delivering it in return for Indian support for war. The talks failed.

In response, Gandhi launched the 'Quit India' movement – another campaign of civil disobedience that included people leaving their jobs and, importantly, Indians refusing to join the British Army. At a major speech in August 1942, Gandhi called on Indians to 'do or die' and 'act as an independent nation'.[10] Less than 24 hours later, he was arrested and imprisoned, as were the majority of the Congress leadership. It was a strategic move.

Indians took to the streets up and down the country in response. This was followed by acts of sabotage against the apparatus of British rule, including power lines, transport links and colonial buildings, but the movement subsided within a year.

A breakaway movement from the Indian National Congress emerged. Former Congress leader Subhash Chandra Bose formed his own political party, and then an army that co-operated with the Japanese to challenge British power militarily. He formed a government-in-exile in Japanese-controlled territory, fought the British directly in Burma, and even briefly captured and ruled two sets of Indian islands, the Andaman and Nicobar islands, which were renamed Shahid ('Martyr') and Swaraj ('Home Rule'). Like Gandhi's Quit India movement, Bose's Indian National Army was ultimately defeated by the overwhelming physical military power of the British. However, public sympathy for the Indian National Army was rather higher amongst the Indian population than it was amongst the British occupiers. In 1946, when captured INA soldiers were tried by the British, solidarity demonstrations took place across India.

This time the discontent did not only manifest itself in the streets. The years following the Second World War saw significant resistance from Indians within the British Indian Army and Royal Indian Navy. On 18 February 1946, sailors in Mumbai went on strike, initially in protest at poor conditions, then at the racist attitudes of their British superiors. The rebellion spread across India, until it reached a peak of 20,000 sailors participating. The ships raised three flags – those of the Indian National Congress, the Muslim League and the Communist Party of India. Once again the strikes were widely supported in India, with solidarity demonstrations, a general strike in Mumbai, and strikes in the air force and police force.[11]

Despite their flags being flown, the mutinies did not win the support of the Indian National Congress or the Muslim League. What the mutinies did do was to close the triangle and undermine Britain's physical power, to add to the way that Gandhi's campaigns helped to undermine British idea power and economic power. Furthermore, they delivered the message that, if Britain did not hand over power to the Indian National Congress and the Muslim League, a far more radical alternative – much more threatening to Britain's interests – would grow in popularity.

In the end, after strikes, non-cooperation, mutinies, sabotage and civil disobedience, Gandhi's early observation that the oppressors cannot rule without the consent of the oppressed was proved to be correct. A letter from British Prime Minister Clement Attlee to Foreign Secretary Ernest Bevin in 1947 showed how years of Counterpower tactics had combined to make imperial rule in India no longer tenable. He wrote: 'We have always governed India through the Indians. Without the tens of thousands of lesser functionaries, we could not carry on. In a typical district of one or two million population it is quite common for there to be only one or two white officials... It would be quite impossible, even if you could find the men, for a few hundred British to administer against the active opposition of the whole of the politically minded population.'[12]

Britain negotiated its exit from India in 1947, eager to avoid the prospect of being forced to make – in Attlee's words – an 'ignominious scuttle'. Idea Counterpower, Economic Counterpower and Physical Counterpower – most of it nonviolent – had eventually won the campaign. Although there is a case to made that 'direct rule by white men in pith helmets has been traded for indirect dominion by white men in pinstripes',[13] India's successful independence movement nevertheless created the first major cracks in an empire that at one point had controlled territory home to a third of the world's population.

Even to begin a list of people influenced by Gandhi's methods is to begin a list of some of the most respected activists of the 20th century. Aung San Suu Kyi, Kwame Nkrumah, Julius Nyerere,

Martin Luther King and Nelson Mandela are only some of them. This prompts the important question: what can we learn?

Lessons from India

A number of books have been written seeking to make recommendations for other movements based on the success of the movement in India. One of the earliest was Richard B Gregg's *The Power of Non-Violence*, released in 1935, which in its 1960 reprint had a foreword by Martin Luther King.[14] But even the title implies a common misconception shared by a number of campaigners – namely that nonviolence is in itself a form of power. Gregg goes so far as to claim that if a victim 'accepts blow after blow, showing no sign of fear or resentment' the attacker will 'plunge forward as it were into a new world of values'. As the following chapters will show, there are certainly examples of elements of the establishment changing sides in the face of principled opposition. But, as future chapters will also show, this is more likely to happen if the movement uses Counterpower.

There is a difference between pacifism and passive-ism. This is shown in Gene Sharp's influential pamphlet *From Dictatorship to Democracy*, in which he calls upon the reader to identify the Achilles heel of the government it is seeking to bring down and thereby to undermine the regime's sources of power. As part of this, he declares that 'by placing confidence in violent means, one has chosen the very type of struggle with which the oppressors nearly always have superiority.'[15] His advice has been read by liberation movements from Serbia to Egypt with considerable success. There is no doubt that nonviolent action can be powerful. But it is through the application of Counterpower that nonviolent strategy succeeds.

In physics, power is the rate at which energy is converted. Political power can be thought of in a similar way. In physics we can speak of thermal energy, potential energy, kinetic energy, and so on. In some ways there are parallels. Exploitation and oppression lead to things heating up (thermal energy), and everyone has the power within them to do something about it (potential energy). This can be transferred into the power of a movement (kinetic energy), which can make change happen. Gandhi discovered that the physical violence of the state can be challenged by transforming the potential power of the Indian people into Economic Counterpower and Idea Counterpower, without the need for armed revolution.

Not every movement that uses Counterpower succeeds – whether violent or otherwise. In fact a great many have not succeeded in all of their aims, although most concerted applications of Counterpower have at least led to partial victories. In order to understand better why some movements have been more successful than others, we need to look at the tactics that power élites use to repel Counterpower.

1 Peter Ackerman and Jack DuVall, *A Force More Powerful: A Century of Nonviolent Conflict*, St Martin's Press, New York, 2000. **2** It was renamed the British East India Company at a later date. **3** Tomas Munro, quoted in Ackerman and DuVall, op cit. **4** Quoted in Lance Collins and Dominique La Pierre, *Freedom at Midnight*, Simon and Schuster, New York, 1975. **5** Known as the Simon Commission. **6** Quoted in *The Hindu*, 'The Great Dandi March: 80 years after', nin.tl/m6rSqK **7** Besant differed with Gandhi on whether to support the First World War, which she opposed. **8** Annie Besant, *An Autobiography*, Fisher Unwin, 1893. **9** MN Roy, *Labour Monthly*, nin.tl/IGfvhS **10** Gandhi 'Quit India' speech, 1942, available online at emersonkent. com/speeches/quit_india.htm **11** Lion Agarwal, *Freedom Fighters of India*, Ishar, Delhi, 2008. **12** Letter from Clement Attlee to Ernest Bevin, 2 Jan 1947, stored at the British Library. **13** Chris Brazier, 'The Radical 20th Century', in *The No-Nonsense Guide to World History*, New Internationalist, third edition, 2010. **14** Richard B Gregg, *The Power of Non-Violence*, James Clark & Co, London, 1935. **15** Gene Sharp, *From Dictatorship to Democracy*, Committee for the Restoration of Democracy in Burma, Bangkok, 1993.

3

How governments respond to Counterpower

'It is not power that corrupts but fear. Fear of losing power corrupts those who wield it and fear of the scourge of power corrupts those who are subject to it.'

Aung San Suu Kyi

Politicians often bemoan people's lack of interest in politics. When they do so, they are usually bemoaning the lack of people supporting *their* politics. Because when a real political movement rises to challenge a government, that government will do everything it can to hold the people concerned back. Governments will try discrediting the movement, smearing it, co-opting it, dividing and ruling it, or – if all that fails – crushing it. In general, it would seem that the greater the strength of the Counterpower movement, the greater is the repressiveness of the government response.

At the time of writing, television footage of soldiers firing on peaceful demonstrators in the Middle East is shocking the world. Yet by so doing governments are repeating a tactic that has been used against dissidents for many years. We saw it when Burmese democracy protesters were shot at both in 1988 and 2007 and in China's response to the student-led protests in Tiananmen Square in 1989. The British response to civil-rights protests in Northern Ireland in 1972 is known as 'Bloody Sunday' after demonstrators were shot in Derry. This is just one of at least seven dates in different countries that have become known by the same name when protests have been suppressed – including the day in 1905 when the armed forces of the Russian Tsar shot at protesters outside the Winter Palace in St Petersburg.

This list only scratches the surface of the times that campaigns using Counterpower have been met with brute force. Such explicit uses of force are usually only utilized when coercion through ideology or economics has failed. It was India's independence hero Mohandas Gandhi who is widely credited with perhaps the most famous summary of how those in authority respond when faced with Counterpower movements: 'First they ignore you, then they laugh at you, then they fight you, then you win.' This may be a version of a longer quotation by the US trade unionist Nicholas Klein, who in 1914 declared: 'First they ignore you. Then they ridicule you. And then they attack you and want to burn you. And then they build monuments to you.' Both are instructive.

This chapter will interrogate this rhetoric by looking at three movements of the 20th century. It would seem that Klein and Gandhi were right about campaigners being ignored, laughed at and fought. However, the historical evidence suggests that there is no inevitability about the eventual victory. Governments and other sources of élite power have a whole raft of tactics available to them that they use to respond to Counterpower movements. Only by understanding them can we overcome them. That is what this chapter seeks to do.

First they ignore you

The power to ignore a movement is possibly the most important and least understood aspect of idea power. It was Peter Bachrach and Morton Baratz who introduced the notion of what they called *non-decision making* to political science. What they meant by this was the ability of the powerful to suppress and restrict the scope of decision making.[1]

Those who dominate a society have a whole range of tools available to them to keep certain issues off the agenda. They can deny that there is a problem; they can concede that there is a problem but declare that the maintenance of the problematic situation is necessary in the context of a bigger 'demon'; or, most insidious of all, they can declare that something is already being done about a certain problem while actually doing the exact opposite.[2]

The all-time global accolade for non-decision making must be awarded to the governments around the world that have successively failed to agree on realistic action to tackle what many consider the biggest threat to humanity as a whole: climate change.

Scientists have known about the greenhouse effect for more than 150 years.[3] For at least 50 years we have known that global warming is caused by humans. In the context of a broader environmental view, the NASA scientist James Lovelock brought some attention to global warming as part of his 'Gaia Hypothesis' in the 1960s, in which he argued that the earth operates as a self-regulating organism, which human activity is altering.[4] However, governments ignored the impending threat.

The first large campaign against global warming was launched in 1988 by the environmental campaign group Friends of the Earth. This followed the front-page news coverage attained by another NASA scientist – James Hansen. He informed a congressional committee that the cause of the drought that had hit the US that year was global warming. And it was going to get worse.

Stewart Boyle, a campaigner who had tried to persuade green NGOs to adopt the issue earlier than they did, summed up the problem as follows: 'Most environmental groups concentrate on a single issue with sharply focused campaigns. The greenhouse effect was just too big and too all-embracing for this approach to work.[5]

Reducing CO_2 to the extent that most climate scientists agree we must implies a very different model of economics and society from the one we currently have. It suggests that there must be limits to production and consumption which result in the release of CO_2. A society that uses less and less is difficult to achieve in the context of an economic system based on consuming more and more. Similarly, it is difficult to achieve a society in which limited resources are shared further when the economic paradigm breeds individualism. So there is a fundamental disconnect between ecological imperatives and the ideology of neoliberalism that began to dominate governments in North America and Europe in the 1980s.*

This was a problem faced by the North American NGOs that were invited to give evidence to the first major meeting of governments and scientists on the issue in 1988 – named the 'Toronto Conference on the Changing Atmosphere'. In his account of events, the environment journalist Fred Pearce writes that, although the best scientific evidence of the time pointed to the need for a CO_2 reduction of at least 50 per cent, the NGOs present did not propose this, because their

---

* It also implies a different model from what some at the time called 'Really Existing Socialism'. In its 70-year life the Soviet Union pumped out about 10 per cent of total CO_2 emissions due to its reliance on heavy industry. Trotsky boasted that 'The proper goal of Communism is the domination of nature by technology, and the domination of technology by planning, so that raw materials of nature will yield to mankind all that it needs and more besides'. However, ecosocialists such as John Bellamy Foster and Derek Wall have sought to reclaim Marx for ecology by pointing out Marx's observation that 'capitalist production disturbs the metabolic interaction between man and the earth; all progress in capitalist agriculture is progress in the art, not only of robbing the worker, but of robbing the soil'. While, perhaps out of necessity, Cuba has had some success in moving away from a reliance on oil.

assessment was that it would not be accepted.[5] Instead, they proposed a 20-per-cent cut by the end of the century, and the necessary 50-per-cent cut some time in the future. The conference agreed. They gave the impression of having made a decision. In fact they had made a non-decision. The necessary changes didn't even make it onto the agenda.

The conference did, however, pave the way for the Intergovernmental Panel on Climate Change (IPCC). This expert group of scientists from across the world soon clarified that to avoid the worst effects of climate change 80-per-cent CO_2 cuts would be necessary.[6] The chasm between the advice of the scientists and the actions of politicians was astounding.

In the 1970s, a number of green NGOs and political parties were established whose popularity grew due to concerns about animal habitats, acid rain, landfill and other environmental issues. When the issue of global warming catapulted into the public consciousness, their popularity bloomed. The growth in concern is perhaps most measurable in the rise in ballots cast for green political parties. Following the European election of 1989, the Green Party in the European Parliament had enough elected MEPs to form their own group for the first time. In the UK, the Green Party received 15 per cent of the vote – a meteoric rise from their 1984 result of just 1 per cent. This did not translate into their getting any representatives into the Parliament, due to an electoral system designed to keep small parties out. It did, however, deliver a message to mainstream political parties: if they wanted to get elected, they needed to give the impression that they were doing something about global warming.

In 1992, governments saw the perfect opportunity: the Earth Summit in Rio de Janeiro, Brazil. To great public acclaim, more than 100 world leaders attended. Each was given the opportunity to make serious-sounding speeches about their concern for the planet. They then proceeded to make a series of non-decisions. The most publicized at the time was *Agenda 21:* a blueprint for sustainable development with little or no means with which to deliver it. Another non-decision was that, rather than agreeing on realistic CO_2 cuts, they would set up a process by which to do so. Or, as it transpired, by which not to do so. That process was called the United Nations Framework Convention on Climate Change (UNFCCC).[7] At the time of writing, in 2011, 16 'Conference of Parties' summits of the UNFCCC have taken place. None has produced a decision that climate scientists have declared capable of stopping climate change.

One of the newspaper journalists to follow the workings of the UNFCCC and IPCC most closely is George Monbiot of *The Guardian* newspaper in Britain. He writes: 'The drafting of reports by the world's pre-eminent group of climate scientists is an odd process. For many months scientists contributing to the Intergovernmental Panel on Climate Change tussle over the evidence. Nothing gets published unless it achieves consensus. This means that the panel's reports are extremely conservative – even timid. It also means that they are as trustworthy as a scientific document can be. Then, when all is settled among the scientists, the politicians sweep in and seek to excise from the summaries anything which threatens their interests.'[8]

Amongst politicians' interests are their funds. This is especially important in the US. Since 1992, 90 per cent of elections to Congress have been won by the candidate with the most money. In the first decade of the new millennium, companies from the oil and gas industry spent over $100 million on US politicians.[9]

The role of corporations in such non-decision making on climate change has on occasion been quite blatant. For instance, in 2003, Phil Cooney, a White House staff member previously employed as an oil-industry lobbyist, made hundreds of changes to reports on climate change produced by the US Environmental Protection Agency. Despite the fact he had no scientific training, Cooney inserted clauses suggesting that there were serious scientific doubt about global warming, and ultimately watered down the US position. Two days after the story broke in the *New York Times*, Cooney resigned. A few days after that, he was offered another job in the oil industry.[10]

This was just one instance of many that show corporations intervening to ensure that no decisions are made that might harm their profits. The first response is generally to continue denying that there is a problem. In 1993, for example, a group called 'TASSC', an acronym for 'The Advancement of Sound Science Coalition' was founded. Although the name suggests a grassroots group of concerned scientists, it was no such thing. The 'group' initially sought to sow doubt about the belief that smoking caused respiratory disease, aided by a substantial grant from the Philip Morris cigarette corporation. Then it began to diversify and argue that the science behind climate change was not yet proven. In 1998 the organization started receiving money the from the oil giant Exxon.[10]

TASSC's employee Steve Milloy was awarded a regular slot on Fox News. TASSC is, however, only one of numerous organizations funded by oil companies in the service of denying the impacts of climate change. Amongst them are many with innocent-sounding names – such as the 'Global Climate Coalition', 'National Environmental Policy Institute' and the 'National Wetlands Coalition'. Yet their effect is to stymie the drive for effective environmental regulation. And the problem goes far beyond outspoken media outlets such as Fox News. The impression that a number of organizations oppose the genuine green groups' concerns has meant that even media sources that strive for 'balance' have felt the need to feature deniers of climate change when reporting. The result has been to sow doubt in the mind of the public, and to encourage yet more non-decision making by governments.

Another approach by corporations to the issue was to claim that they already had the solutions. This began in the late 1980s, when a whole range of so-called 'environmentally friendly' products began to hit the shelves. For example, BP launched a new brand of 'Supergreen' unleaded petrol which it claimed 'caused no pollution to the environment'. The period also saw the rise of 'green' investment funds. A series of problems with these has been uncovered. For example, it was discovered that one such fund had incinerators in its portfolio.[5]

Another questionable green product dreamed up by business is the notion of 'carbon trading' – the idea that some countries or companies should be able to keep polluting and pay others to make CO_2 reductions elsewhere. The idea was invented in the US, where Vice-President Al Gore was then persuaded that the Kyoto Protocol could not be signed without it. Despite the fact that until just over a year previously they had refused to publicly acknowledge the link between their core business and climate change, BP began to trial carbon trading internally, led by a staff member named John Mogford. His wife Margaret Mogford – also an employee in the fossil-fuel sector – was seconded to the UK Department for the Environment in 2000 to develop the first multi-industry carbon-trading scheme in the world. When it was trialed two years later, BP was awarded £18.9 million (then $27.6 million) in incentive payments.[11] After more lobbying by both UK government and oil companies, the EU adopted a similar system. In five years of the EU Emissions Trading Scheme, the participating companies reduced their greenhouse gas emissions by just one third of one per cent.[9] Meanwhile, credits were over-allocated to industry. Instead of making the polluter pay, the polluter was paid. Once again, real solutions stayed off the agenda.[12]

Given the unlikelihood of governmental change, some green campaigners decided to focus on encouraging individual behavior change. But a recent study by the World Wildlife Fund sheds light on the limits of this approach, finding evidence that such initiatives 'can serve to deflect pressure for government to adopt ambitious and potentially unpopular policies and regulations; it allows businesses to claim they are contributing meaningfully to engaging a problem such as climate change through the sale of compact fluorescent light bulbs or washing-lines; and it helps to relieve environmental NGOs of the (potentially upsetting) obligation to draw attention to the full scale and urgency of global environmental problems.'[13]

Thus, in different ways over a period of decades, governments have consciously or otherwise engaged in non-decision making on the issue of climate change. Chapter 7 will look at the tactics adopted by the global justice movement from 1999 onwards to address this. But after ignoring campaigners, governments have another tactic to use when faced with Counterpower movements: ridicule.

Then they ridicule you

In the second stage, Gandhi suggested that 'they laugh at you' and Klein suggested that they 'ridicule you'. The French philosopher Michel Foucault argued that, by creating notions of 'common knowledge', élites in society are able to create definitions of right and wrong. By extension, this gives élites the power to define what kind of behavior is 'normal' and what kind is 'deviant'. The analysis applies well to governments using their power against movements that challenge them. The ability to 'discipline and punish' is a kind of physical power, but it has a far greater impact – the ability to define who is and is not a 'criminal'.

At the outbreak of the First World War, patriotism and nationalism were the dominant ideologies on both sides. Faced with such a pervasive paradigm, the early peace movement faced an immense challenge. By disciplining and punishing anti-war campaigners, governments were able to label them as deviants.

The human cost of what was known at the time as the 'Great War' was vast. There is no definitive number of the deaths, but 10 million is a conservative estimate. The conflict was dominated by trench warfare, as soldiers dug holes in the ground so as to be out of the line of fire from the opposite side. At intervals, men would be ordered out of the trenches to charge towards the other side, often suffering devastating losses. There were periodic massacres, including the Battle of the Somme, during which more than a million young men from France, Germany and Britain were killed. On a single day in July 1916, 58,000 people were mown down by machine gunfire, of whom 20,000 were killed, after their commanders ordered them to invade German trenches.[14] The result of the Somme offensive, and all of this loss of life, was that Allied troops gained 10 kilometers of land.

The idea power commanded by governments at war often builds on and extends the concepts promoted during peacetime and previous wars. This was most certainly the case during World War One. Governments, in concert with mainstream newspapers, churches and establishment figures, romanticized and honored those willing to sign up and fight. They emphasized notions of patriotism, nationalism and empire, which resonated with the masses, having been built up over centuries.

A complex web of alliances was established in the years prior to the war. When Archduke Franz Ferdinand of Austria was assassinated on 28 June 1914, the incident triggered a series of conflicts that quickly pulled a number of countries into the conflict. As governments one by one declared war, each argued that doing so was necessary for national defense – Germany against Russia, France against Germany, Britain to defend Belgium, and so on.[15] Every government promulgated the idea that the purpose of the war was to defend democracy and the national way of life.

Even as the opening shots of war were fired, this idea power alone overwhelmed the leaders of the mainstream anti-war movement. Although the Social Democratic Party of Germany (SPD), the French Socialist Party and the British Labour Party had all stated their opposition during the build-up to war, they then changed their minds. The Democrat Woodrow Wilson was elected President of the United States on a manifesto which included a promise to stay out of the war. He too later reneged on his previous stance.

Some people saw the war as a bloody struggle for resources and territory. There is certainly evidence for this view. In a much-read book of the time, the investigative journalist ED Morel described how the German stationing of a warship off the coast of the French protectorate of Morocco was a key moment in the lead-up to war.[16] The struggles between Russia and Austria over the control of Bosnia are a better-known factor. When the war was under way, French and British troops took control of the German colonies of Togoland, Cameroon and what was then known as German East Africa – now Tanzania, Rwanda and Burundi. The British army also used the opportunity to invade and lay claim to Palestine, Trans-Jordan and Mesopotamia (modern-day Iraq).* This has had knock-on effects for the region ever since.

In response, there was a growth in groups opposed to war rooted in the left. In Germany, for example, Rosa Luxemburg broke away from the SPD to form the Spartacus League – a reference to the famous leader of the Roman slave rebellions. In the US, the Socialist Party of America grew in popularity and the prominent anarchists Emma Goldman and Alexander Berkman established the No Conscription League.[17] In Britain, Ramsay MacDonald resigned as chair of the Labour Party and established the Union of Democratic Control, which called for parliamentary votes on foreign policy, and advocated that, at the end of the war, negotiations and peace terms should be arranged in such a way so as to decrease the likelihood of future hostilities. Meanwhile, fellow Independent Labour Party member Fenner Brockway co-founded the 'No More War Fellowship'.

---

*When the British army arrived in Baghdad in 1917 the commanding officer declared 'our armies do not come into your cities and your lands as conquerors or enemies but as liberators'. The way the British ruled, in particular with relation to the region's oil, did not reflect this early statement.

Another strand of resistance was based in religion. Many Christians reasoned that killing people was incompatible with Jesus' teaching, and that spiritual truth, or God's guidance, was of a higher order than that of national leaders. It was in such a spirit that the English Quaker Henry Hodgkin and German Lutheran Friedrich Siegmund-Schultze pledged to one another on the platform of a railway station in Cologne that 'We are one in Christ and can never be at war'. They kept their pledge by establishing 'The Fellowship of Reconciliation', an international pacifist organization based on Christian principles.[18] By 1915, the Fellowship of Reconciliation had spread to the US.

In theory, of course, it would be impossible to pursue any war if enough people refused to fight. But simply imprisoning anti-war figures could make martyrs of them and could possibly increase pro-peace sentiment. Alongside the punishment there was a skilful propaganda campaign playing to nationalist sentiment that marginalized opponents of the war.

This was clearly reflected in the recruitment posters of the time. On the outbreak of war, the British government commissioned a poster featuring Lord Kitchener in which he points outwards toward the reader with the words 'Your Country Needs You'. It was later adopted in the US with the picture changed to 'Uncle Sam'. As the anti-recruitment campaign grew, another poster was commissioned, so iconic that, like the Kitchener poster, it is still recognized today. It depicts a guilty-looking middle-aged man looking into the distance. At his feet his son plays with toy soldiers, and his daughter asks him 'Daddy, what did YOU do in the Great War?'

This came alongside the use of physical power against dissenters. In April 1918, 101 members of the anti-war Industrial Workers of the World were put on trial. Every one of them was found 'guilty' and sentenced to prison. The following year, 249 Russian-born activists were arrested and deported, including Emma Goldman and Alexander Berkman. Peace campaigners of US origin were also rounded up. Then, in 1920, some 4,000 people who had been born abroad were arrested in the US, many of whom were then forced to walk through the streets together in pairs, chained and handcuffed.[14]

The British government had pursued a similar approach. Despite the reformist politics and constitutionalist methods of the Union of Democratic Control (UDC), the press led a campaign against it. In April 1915, the *Daily Express* printed 'wanted' posters of its most prominent members – Ramsay MacDonald and ED Morel. The *John Bull* magazine went further and demanded that MacDonald should be tried by court-martial and condemned as 'an aider and abetter of the King's enemies'.[19] MacDonald lost his seat at the following election. Morel suffered a worse fate. Amid the public attention, his house was raided by the authorities. When it was discovered that he had technically broken the law by posting a UDC pamphlet to a friend living abroad, he was sentenced to prison for six months.

The government encouraged people to shun anti-war activists – and suggested that women give white feathers (a symbol of cowardice) to men not enlisted. On the streets, anti-war activists faced taunts of 'Coward', 'Shirker', and 'Conchie' for refusing to join the forces.

In an anthology of anti-war voices stored at the Imperial War Museum, Harold Bing, a conscientious objector, recalls how difficult life became: 'On the whole, apart from a few friends and sympathizers, people's attitudes towards me were distinctly hostile. This would be the ostracism of neighbors who knew I was going to appeal to be a CO or a critical attitude of my employers who terminated my contract after my tribunal and refused to reinstate me.'[18] Many peace campaigners lost their jobs. Even Bertrand Russell, a renowned philosopher, was dismissed from his post at Cambridge University.

The war played hard on Keir Hardie. In the early days he made efforts to organize a Europe-wide strike against the hostilities. But the call was not taken up and many within the very party he had helped to found came to regard him as a traitor. He died a short while later. In her memoirs Sylvia Pankhurst recalls that 'the great slaughter, the rending of the bonds of international fraternity, on which he had built his hopes, had broken him.'[20]

In most countries the anti-war cause was hampered by the pervasive ideology of nationalism but in Ireland and Canada (particularly Quebec) nationalist sentiment aided the anti-war cause. In both cases the vibrant campaigns against conscription represented important steps in the independence movements of those countries. In the former colony of Australia there were divides in opinion along the lines of religion, class and to some extent gender. In two referenda, the population (narrowly) voted against conscription.

In Russia, anti-war campaigning had a very different character, as it fused with broader economic concerns and identification with class to bring about the downfall of the Tsarist regime. At the beginning of the war, much of the country rallied behind the Tsar, but, as social conditions in the country plummeted, people marched out of the factories on strike. Their first demand was for bread, then for an end to the war, then for an end to the undemocratic rule of the Tsar. The turning point came when soldiers were ordered to fire on the demonstrators. They refused, and instead decided to march alongside them. The Tsar opted to make his way to Petrograd (the new name for St Petersburg) but was obstructed by revolutionaries. Sitting impotent in his railway carriage, he was advised to abdicate. He did.

A situation of dual power emerged, with a provisional government on one hand and committees of workers and soldiers on the other – the soviets. Despite pleas by the provisional government for troops to keep fighting, radical influence grew in the ranks. As new demonstrations took place in Petrograd, two million Russian soldiers deserted between February and October 1917. On 24 October 1917, forces of the Petrograd Soviet took over government buildings in the city. The following day, mutinous sailors from Kronstadt assisted revolutionary forces to take control of the Winter Palace, Russia's seat of power. The new government negotiated its exit from the First World War.*

Despite differences in politics, events gave confidence to class-based movements in other countries too – most notably Germany. In October 1918, sailors in Kiel mutinied and formed their own soviets. By November the rebellion had spread. A general strike was called in Berlin and armed groups took to the streets. According to Peter Nettl's account in his biography of Rosa Luxemburg, the tipping point came when Spartacus League leader Karl Liebknecht gave a speech proclaiming the Socialist Republic. He writes: 'When news of these events reached the Reichstag, where the SPD caucus was in permanent session, Scheidemann was persuaded to declare the Democratic Republic then and there to prevent a complete Spartacus takeover'.[21]

In Scotland, too, a number of strikes in munitions factories took place alongside mass demonstrations on the streets in what has come to be known as 'Red Clydeside'. In the end both German and Scottish initiatives were brutally put down. Rosa Luxemburg and Karl Liebknecht were murdered in 1919, following a further uprising by workers. The Scottish protests were suppressed by placing tanks on the streets of Glasgow.

The cases of Red Clydeside and the Spartacist Uprising present clear examples of governments moving beyond ridicule

---

* The Bolsheviks were not, however, a party of peace. One of Lenin's pre-revolutionary slogans was 'turn imperialist war into civil war'. After the events of October 1917 the Russian Army was renamed the Red Army as it continued the fight against a new force – the White Army of counter-revolutionaries. The new regime was forced to introduce conscription in 1918. As the new regime suppressed dissent within the country, leaders found themselves in disagreement with many international figures who had initially supported the revolution, including Sylvia Pankhurst, Emma Goldman and Rosa Luxemburg. A discussion of how the methods of change influence the eventual state of affairs is included in this book's conclusion.

and fighting opposition movements outright. However, in all countries – Scotland and Germany included – the state's capacity to discipline and punish was used to attempt to prevent resistance from escalating to such an extent that it could seriously challenge the interests of the government.[22] The historian Howard Zinn sums this up in *A People's History of the United States* when he writes that the courts and jails were used 'to reinforce the idea that certain ideas, certain kinds of resistance, could not be tolerated'.

Nevertheless, the anti-war campaigners played a part in the birth of a movement promoting concepts of peace and justice in opposition to the dominant ideologies of imperialism and nationalism. When they began, their Idea Counterpower was still small, but as it has slowly grown, it has had an important effect. In the years following the First World War, novels like Erich Maria Remarque's *All Quiet on the Western Front* and Ernest Hemingway's *A Farewell to Arms*, plays like RC Sherriff's *Journey's End* and memoirs such as Robert Graves' *Goodbye to All That* began to reflect the true nature of life in the trenches and the futility of war. These ideas were suppressed by governments and ignored by the media while the war was going on – indeed the title *All Quiet on the Western Front* is a reference to how the war was reported at home even while untold suffering was taking place on the frontline.

Six members of the International Fellowship of Reconciliation have won the Nobel Peace Prize over the years, including two who feature in this book: US civil rights leader Martin Luther King Jr and South African anti-apartheid campaigner Chief Albert Luthuli. Furthermore, the Society of Friends (Quakers) was awarded the prize in 1947, in part because of the role of the Friends Ambulance Unit, established in World War One and re-established during World War Two. Bertrand Russell was also awarded a Nobel Prize – although his was for literature – partly in recognition of his longstanding humanitarianism.

In 1985, a statue of conscientious objector Fenner

Brockway was erected in London's Red Lion Square to mark a life that also included the co-founding of the anti-poverty organization War on Want and campaigns against colonialism. In 1998, Britons whom soldiers had shot as punishment for 'desertion' or 'cowardice' were honored at London's Cenotaph for the first time.

For the most part, governments attempted to ridicule the anti-war movements of World War One. As resistance movements began to exert their Counterpower, the government fought back with physical power too. But fighting a movement does not simply mean physically repressing it. As we will see from the next example, in the 1980s, British Prime Minister Margaret Thatcher used every kind of ideological, economic and physical power available to her to fight the Counterpower of trade unionists. How she did so is revealed in the story of the Miners' Strike.

Then they fight you

One of the most famous works of political philosophy on the subject of power is Machiavelli's 16th-century masterpiece *The Prince*. The book was written as guidance to a ruler seeking to maintain power and has informed many leaders through the ages. In it, Machiavelli advises that: 'A prince ought to have no other aim or thought, nor select anything else for his study, than war and its rules and discipline'. He also advises that: 'A prince ought to have two fears, one from within, on account of his subjects, the other from without, on account of external powers.'[23]

It is not clear whether Thatcher read *The Prince* or not. However, in one of her speeches, she echoed these words of Machiavelli when she proclaimed 'In the Falklands we had to fight the enemy without. Here we have the enemy within, which is much more difficult to fight and more dangerous to liberty'.[24]

Her approach was simultaneously to isolate, divide and rule, smear, and ultimately crush the labor movement, beginning with the mineworkers. Despite the resolve and sustained

Counterpower of the mineworkers and their supporters, the government succeeded in mobilizing more power.

Thatcher was a long-time opponent of the National Union of Mineworkers (NUM). She had been a government minister in 1972, when trade-union action by miners had played a central role in weakening the Conservative government of Edward Heath. The climax had been a tense standoff involving the picketing of a coking plant in Birmingham by 10,000 striking workers. The result had been victory for the trade unionists and humiliation for the government. Following more strikes, Heath called an election in 1974, asking 'Who runs Britain?' He lost.

The organizer of the 1972 picket had been a Yorkshire man named Arthur Scargill. Nine years later, he became president of the NUM. Thatcher never forgot. When Thatcher's Conservative government took on Scargill's NUM it wasn't only political. There was a personal element involved too.

In the wake of the 1974 defeat, Conservative MP Nicholas Ridley began work on the plan that would eventually overpower the miners. He recommended that a future Conservative government should trigger a strike, but only after building coal stocks, encouraging coal imports, ensuring that coal hauliers were non-unionized, and training up a new, more mobile breed of police officers to put down resistance.[25] Every one of these tactics was used by the Conservative government in its eventual battle with the mineworkers.

Machiavelli emphasized the importance of preparedness for war. When Margaret Thatcher was elected prime minister in 1979, she played her hand carefully. During her first term, she used the idea power of speeches to build antipathy towards trade unions, then built on this antipathy to pass new anti-union legislation. She implemented Ridley's plan by building coal stocks, encouraging coal imports and training new squads of riot police. She also sought to diversify Britain's energy mix, by initiating a 'dash for gas' and – with much public subsidy – investing in nuclear power. But she did not pick a major fight with the miners straight away. For the time being, they were too strong. In the 1980s, 80 per cent of Britain's electricity still came from burning British coal.[25] A national stoppage, without the necessary preparation, could have forced the government to climb down within weeks.

The major battle of Thatcher's first term was not at home but 250 nautical miles off the coast of South America, in the waters surrounding the Falklands – a cluster of islands in the South Atlantic Ocean with a population of just 3,000, and oil and gas reserves in the surrounding sea. Despite the move towards decolonization that had characterized the mid-20th century, these islands remained in British possession.

On 2 April 1982, Argentina reclaimed the Falklands, which it calls the Malvinas. In response, Thatcher ordered UK gunships to re-invade the British Overseas Territory in a conflict that eventually took the lives of 655 Argentinean and 255 British soldiers. Despite the deaths, the war boosted Thatcher's idea power. Before the battle the Prime Minister's personal approval ratings stood at a lowly 25 per cent. Over the duration of the war, this more than doubled.[26] The small anti-war movement was not helped by the decision of Michael Foot – then leader of the Labour Party – to support the invasion, despite his record as a peace campaigner. The Conservatives won the 1983 general election by a large margin. Thatcher was finally in a position to take on her most hated enemy.

In 1984, when coal stocks were at their highest and the winter was over, the government-owned National Coal Board announced that 20,000 mineworkers would be made redundant. By 5 March miners in Yorkshire had successfully balloted to strike, followed by other areas, one by one. Within a day, half of the miners in the country were on strike. Within a fortnight this rose to 80 per cent. Pickets became a regular occurrence outside collieries. In addition – remembering the tactics used so successfully in 1972 – pickets were dispatched to coking plants to heighten the Counterpower the movement could wield. What ensued was a long and bitter nationwide industrial confrontation, which lasted a year.

Leaks that came to light after the strike reveal that Margaret Thatcher personally authorized the government spying center GCHQ to run a 'Get Scargill' campaign.[25] A network of spies and *agents provocateurs* reported back to government.

Smear stories were seized upon by many media outlets. In one case the BBC went so far as to edit film so that it looked as though picketers had initiated attacks on police, when evidence later revealed that quite the opposite had happened.[27] It was in 1991 – long after the dispute was over – that the BBC finally apologized, saying that the order had been 'inadvertently reversed'.[28]

Nevertheless, there were moments of resistance. The Rupert Murdoch-owned *Sun* newspaper planned a front page in which miners' leader Arthur Scargill was depicted as Hitler under the headline 'Mine Fuhrer'. In a stunning display of Economic Counterpower in action the print workers refused to process the offensive picture. Instead the newspaper ran with a message across the cover reading: 'Members of the Sun production chapels refused to handle the Arthur Scargill picture and major headline in our story. *The Sun* has decided, reluctantly, to print the story without either.'

The government's tactics against the strikers were, however, not restricted to idea power. It very successfully used its economic power to refuse benefits to those on strike. Communities found their own ways of countering this. Collections took place up and down the country, food kitchens were set up and food deliveries made to the picket lines and to the families of striking miners.

Another use of government economic coercion was more difficult to counter. Mid-strike, the state won a court case against the NUM which resulted in the sequestration of the union's funds. Instead the organization was forced to operate without a bank account, and had to transfer cash from one part of the union to another in bags, boxes and suitcases.

The court case centered on the fact that the NUM did not call a national ballot ahead of the strike. Instead, regions made their own decisions to join or otherwise. Most did so. When Nottinghamshire did not, it handed an unexpected boost to the government's ability to use economic power. Nottinghamshire miners were awarded incentive payments, and their output allowed coal stocks to last for longer than they would have otherwise.[25]

Neil Kinnock, the new leader of the Labour Party (and MP for Islwyn, a coal-mining constituency in South Wales) refused to give his support to the NUM. The Labour and TUC hierarchies quickly rebuked leftwing MP Tony Benn when he stated his view that 'The Labour movement has now got to face the fact that a general strike might become necessary to protect free trade unionism, ballot-box democracy, political freedom and civil liberties in Britain.'[24]

Most flagrant, however, was the use of physical power against the movement. According to the Justice for Mineworkers Campaign, 20,000 NUM campaigners were injured or hospitalized due to their involvement in the dispute. Two people, Joe Green and David Jones, died on the picket line.[29]

Campaigners outside mines and coking plants were periodically forced back by police to allow delivery trucks or armored buses of 'scab' labor into the sites. On 18 June 1984, at the Orgreave Coking Plant in South Yorkshire, the new police tactic of containment was introduced – better known today as 'kettling'. But it did not stop there. Some 8,000 police, with shields, horses and dogs, attacked the picket. It led to the most famous battle of the campaign.

Arthur Scargill himself was injured at Orgreave, by being hit over the head with a riot shield. The police initially tried to deny this by declaring that Scargill had accidentally slipped. The police were no longer able credibly to make this claim when pictures emerged of the incident that backed up Scargill's account.[27]

The state's use of physical power did not stop at straightforward violence. Over the course of the campaign, there were more than 10,000 arrests of striking miners.[24] Many of these arrests were for offenses such as 'actions likely to cause a breach of the peace', 'unlawful assembly' and even the somewhat antiquated law 'watching and besetting'.[30] Many other miners were arrested *en masse* only to be released later without charge. Those who were charged frequently had stringent bail conditions imposed, which limited their capacity to campaign. Some were targeted by 'snatch squads' of police. Others were pushed forward by *agents provocateurs* in the crowds.[31] A few miners were charged with more serious offences such as 'incitement to cause a riot'. These cases invariably collapsed, but not until considerable energy had been diverted from the campaign into the court process.

In 1991, the South Yorkshire Police had to pay half a million pounds (then $890,000) in damages to 39 miners who successfully sued the police for false imprisonment, malicious prosecution, wrongful arrest and assault after having been arrested at Orgreave. It is likely that many more who had had similar experiences had neither the money nor the emotional energy to appeal against their treatment.

To keep the coal coming out of Nottinghamshire, the police prevented many other miners from entering the county. According to the chief constable of Nottinghamshire, 64,508 people were prevented from entering Nottinghamshire in the first 27 days of the strike alone.[24]

Eventually, on 5 March 1985, the miners were effectively starved back to work. Despite their dignified re-entrance, marching behind colliery bands, the determined Counterpower of the movement had been vanquished by the overwhelming power of the state.

That is not to diminish the considerable Counterpower of the movement. Officials had been preparing for a six-month strike, yet the confrontation lasted double that time.

Nor was the campaign without successes. Although the pits were not kept open, the longest-serving miners left their jobs with redundancy packages of £80,000 ($140,000) – almost unheard-of at the time.[25]

In addition, the massive role played by the women in mining communities helped to shift the balance of power in the home. One woman wrote in 1985: 'One of the good things that has come out of this strike, is that there's a lot of marriages that are working one hundred per cent better now... the women aren't doormats any more.'[32] The folk singer Sandra Kerr later wrote and recorded a song about it with women from Staffordshire:

> 'Since the miners' strike has ended, a new life has begun.
> We're different women after all we've seen and done.
> We've learned the world's divided. Now we have made our choice.
> We may have lost our battle but we've found our voice.'

And then you win?

These stories, from the peace movement, the climate movement and the trade union movement, reveal that not every campaign that is ignored and laughed at, wins. Or, at least, not straight away. It must be remembered that each of the three campaigns above represent only chapters in the biographies of movements that have not yet ended. The struggles for peace, trade unionism and a safe climate are alive and well.

Campaigners might find encouragement in the words of South African activist Joe Slovo. More than a decade before the fall of apartheid, he wrote: 'Until the moment of successful revolutionary take-over, each individual act of resistance usually fails... the rare moment in history which makes possible the final victorious revolutionary assault is a compound of a people and a movement with an accumulated heritage of resistance, which, through all the immediate 'failures', perpetuates and reinforces the tradition of struggle.'[33]

In this respect, Richard Dawkins' conception of the 'meme' is useful. The word is used to denote the way that ideas are transferred from one person to another as reflected in art, literature, fashion and politics. There can be no doubt that the memes generated by these past campaigns help inform the knowledge and identity of campaigners today.

While there is much to be learned from looking at campaigns that did not immediately succeed in their principal objectives, there is also a great deal to be learned from a movement that eventually won. The next chapter will therefore examine the campaign against the US war in Vietnam.

1 See Bachrach and Baratz in Mark Haugaard (ed), *Power: A Reader*, Manchester University Press, 2002. **2** These points are drawn broadly from Bill Moyer's Movement Action Plan, 1987. **3** In 1858 the scientist John Tyndall succeeded in providing reliable evidence for the existence of 'The Greenhouse Effect', in turn building on the work of the mathematician Joseph Fourier in 1824, who helped provide a logical explanation for why the earth remained so warm despite its distance from the sun. **4** James Lovelock, ecolo.org/lovelock/lovebioen.htm **5** Fred Pearce, *Green Warriors: The People and the Politics behind the Environmental Revolution*, Bodley Head, London, 1991. **6** Greenpeace, *Chronology of Conferences*, nin.tl/jxvAZw **7** The convention was opened for signature at Rio, although preparation work for it had taken place beforehand. **8** George Monbiot, *The Guardian*, 10 April 2007. **9** Danny Chivers, *The No-Nonsense Guide to Climate Change*, New Internationalist, Oxford, 2011. **10** George Monbiot, *Heat*, Allen Lane, London, 2006, nin.tl/lzFfL2. **11** Platform and Corporate Europe Observatory, *Putting the Fox in Charge of the Henhouse: How BP's Emissions Trading Scheme was Sold to the EU*, nin.tl/jukuis **12** Sarah-Jayne Clifton, *Offsetting - A Dangerous Distraction*, Friends of the Earth nin.tl/mhXqBa **13** WWF, *Simple and Painless? The limitations of spill-over in environmental campaigning*, 2009. **14** Howard Zinn, *A People's History of the United States*, Harper & Row, New York, 1980. **15** Megan Trudell, *Prelude to Revolution*, Socialist Review, 1997. **16** ED Morel, *Ten Years of Secret Diplomacy: An Unheeded Warning*. National Labour Press, London, 1915. **17** Manifesto of the No Conscription League, katesharpleylibrary.net/wpzhxw **18** Lynne Smith (ed), *Voices Against War: A Century of Protest*, Mainstream, Edinburgh, 2009. **19** Spartacus, *The Union of Democratic Control*, nin.tl/kaEebx **20** Excerpt from Sylvia Pankhurst, *The Suffragette Movement*, 1935 at nin.tl/lKUUcR **21** John Peter Nettl, *Rosa Luxemburg*, Oxford University Press, 1969. **22** A response to some of the rumors spread about the Spartacus League, first published in *Die Rote Fahne*, can be found on p454 of Nettl, op cit. **23** Niccolò Machiavelli, *The Prince*, available online at constitution.org/mac/prince14.htm **24** Rob Sewell, *In the Cause of Labour: History of British Trade Unionism*, Wellred, London, 2003. **25** Seamus Milne, *The Enemy Within: The Secret War Against the Miners*, Verso, London, 1994. **26** Naomi Klein, *The Shock Doctrine*, Allen Lane, London, 2007.

27 Mick Duncan, *Lies, Damned Lies and the Press* at workersliberty.org/node/2366 **28** Rhian Jones, 'From Orgreave to the City', *Red Pepper*, Jun 2009, nin.tl/ilsqoJ **29** Justice for Mineworkers Campaign, nin.tl/mmEjWV **30** NCCL, *Civil Liberties and the Miners' Dispute*, 1984. **31** Dave Douglass, *Come and Wet this Truncheon*, Canary Press, 1986. **32** North Yorkshire Women Against Pit Closures, *Strike 84-85*, 1985. **33** Joe Slovo et al, *Southern Africa: The New Politics of Revolution*, Penguin, London, 1976.

4

How the Vietnam War was stopped

'We shall overcome, we shall overcome.'

Charles Albert Tindley

At the turn of the century a gospel preacher wrote a song. In the early 20th century it was taught to union organizers. Then in 1947 it was published in a protest song book. It became the anthem of the civil-rights movement and, as many of the same campaigners provided the impetus for the campaign against the Vietnam War, it formed part of the soundtrack to the biggest peace movement the United States had ever seen. As it traveled, its meaning, words and uses changed. The song was *We Shall Overcome*.

A single song didn't stop the war in Vietnam. But in its verses is an explanation for why the movement against the war ended in success whereas the movements in the previous chapter did not. Encapsulated in the words 'We shall overcome' is the idea of surmounting each problem faced and prevailing over the opponent. The second verse declares 'We'll walk hand in hand' – a statement of solidarity. Transferred to the campaign against the war, this meant escalating Counterpower tactics proportionately and resisting the attempts to divide and rule.

These two lessons can be seen quite clearly in the case of the anti-war movement in the US in the 1960s and 1970s. First it was ignored, then it was ridiculed, then it was fought against. But through escalation and solidarity, the movement eventually won.

The war in Vietnam

The origins of the war in Vietnam stretch back to the late 19th century when France invaded and subjected the country to colonial rule. Vietnam was then occupied by Japan during World War Two. In response, a national liberation movement was established to fight the new invaders. The movement was called the *Vietminh* which translates as the 'League for the Independence of Vietnam'. When the Second World War came to an end in 1945, China and Britain arranged to divide Vietnam up between them. However, before China could take control of the North, as arranged, the Vietminh marched on the northern city of Hanoi. On 2 September 1945, the Democratic Republic of Vietnam declared its independence. At its head was the prominent communist who had led the military campaign – Ho Chi Minh.

British forces occupied the south and assisted French forces to try and reassert control over their former colony. They soon succeeded in driving Ho Chi Minh's troops out of Hanoi. US President Eisenhower worried that were Vietnam to become a communist country, other countries in South East Asia would do likewise 'like dominoes'. Because of this, the US bankrolled the French campaign. The Vietminh in turn won the support of the Chinese government after Mao's Communist Party took charge in 1949.

In 1954, a battle at Dien Bien Phu, near the border with Laos, proved the decisive victory for the Vietnamese. Vietminh troops outmaneuvered the occupiers by carrying heavy artillery into the hills – something the French had presumed impossible.[1] Afterwards, General Vo Nguyen Giap, architect of the Vietminh military strategy, said: 'A poor, feudal nation had beaten a great colonial power... it meant a lot; not just to us, but to people all over the world'.[2]

For most or all of the living memory of people in Vietnam, foreign countries had asserted themselves as rulers of their country. First came France, then Japan, then China and Britain, then France again. Although the Vietnamese had now seen them all off, its problems were not yet over. Now they had another foreign power to deal with – the US.

In the same year that the Vietminh won their battle against the French, the Geneva Conference recognized US-backed Ngo Dinh Diem as ruler of South Vietnam. The Conference stated that free elections must be held across Vietnam in 1956. This never happened, for fear of the result. In Eisenhower's memoirs he revealed that he knew that 'had the elections been held... 80 per cent of the population would have voted for Ho Chi Minh.'[1]

Ngo Dinh Diem's time was characterized by brutal repression of perceived dissidents, including monks. As well as arresting those thought to oppose the regime, Diem's troops destroyed temples and smashed Buddhist shrines. In response, a number of monks, including Thích Quang Dúc, took to the streets of Saigon and set fire to themselves in protest. This was the beginning of the end for Diem's regime, but it was not the end of unelected US-backed leaders in the country. Diem was soon replaced by a series of US-backed military leaders.

In opposition to the regime of Diem, the National Front for the Liberation of South Vietnam (the NLF) was formed in 1960. It was dedicated to redistribution of wealth and an end to foreign domination of the country. These were the forces the US government came to call the 'Viet Cong'.

In 1964 the US sent warships to spy on Vietnam. The story of what happened next heard by most people was that of Secretary of State Robert McNamara, who said 'while on routine patrol in international waters, the US destroyer *Maddox* underwent unprovoked attack'. Subsequent research suggests that at least two aspects of this statement were untrue: the ships were in Vietnamese waters and the CIA had attacked Vietnamese coastal instillations prior to the event. Even the claim that torpedoes were fired has been cast into doubt.[3] Nevertheless the US promoted their version of events as a justification to begin aerial bombing raids. And so a new phase in the national liberation movement's long campaign for independence began.

Over the course of the war in Vietnam, the US dropped a cumulative weight of seven million tons of bombs on the country – almost one bomb for each person in the country. Almost one in ten people in Vietnam – the vast majority of them civilians – were killed as a result of the war. Causes included hunger, landmines and Agent Orange (a defoliant used to destroy the jungle which also burned human skin). More than 50,000 US troops were killed and another 153,329 seriously wounded. At the height of the war, between 65,000 and 70,000 Vietnamese people were held in prison camps. Many were tortured and beaten as US advisors stood by. In a program entitled 'Operation Phoenix', the US executed without trial 20,000 people whom they suspected of being communists. In defense of the action, a pro-war writer later claimed 'Although the Phoenix program did undoubtedly kill or incarcerate many innocent civilians, it did also eliminate many members of the Communist infrastructure.'[3]

Despite this, the resolve of the resistance stayed solid. The NLF's Idea Counterpower was strong, particularly because of the way that the war was seen as a continuation of a long-standing anti-colonial struggle. The government in North Vietnam was able to wield Economic Counterpower by redistributing land – which in turn assisted its popularity. These combined to buoy the Physical Counterpower of Vietnamese troops, further aided by their familiarity with their surroundings. This helps explain the eventual result of the war. But it does not tell the whole story. The pressure on the US government did not only come from within Southeast Asia, but from within the US itself. It is to that campaign that this chapter will now turn.

We shall overcome

Initially, at least, the US attacks on Vietnam won public and political support at home. The US legislature overwhelmingly endorsed the President's desire to take all necessary measures against North Vietnam. The vote in favor of committing US troops was 88 votes to 2 in the Senate and 416 to 0 in the House of Representatives. Soon after the Gulf of Tonkin incident, the Democrat Lyndon B Johnson was elected President. Of the two candidates running, he was seen as the more inclined towards peace. But, despite his domestic concentration on a 'Great Society' project that involved an assault on poverty, in foreign-policy terms he was to turn out to be one of the most murderous presidents in US history. With the electoral process offering no likely route to stopping the war, activists had to employ Counterpower.

The anti-war movement faced many attacks – ideological, physical and economic. Yet by escalating their own tactics, they prevented themselves from being crushed. Through solidarity, they maintained their resilience.

There can be no doubt that when the US first became involved in the war in Vietnam, the government had idea power on its side. In August 1965, polls showed that US support for the War stood at 61 per cent.[3] By 1971, this figure had been reversed, due in no small part to the applied use of Idea Counterpower by the anti-war movement.

Presidential speeches spoke of the justice of US action in Vietnam, describing it as a struggle between 'Communism' and 'Freedom', and even talked (apparently without irony) of 'assisting the government, the people of Vietnam, to maintain their independence'. History may dismiss such rhetoric, but it was effective at the time. As in the case of the First World War, critics of the war attracted opprobrium and were accused of being unpatriotic. The movement found methods of escalation that countered all of these.

The first demonstrations to oppose the war in Vietnam attracted only a few people, who were splattered with paint by pro-war hecklers. But the movement grew. The Student Nonviolent Coordinating Committee, which had played a major role in civil rights campaigning, came out against the war in 1966. Out of the SNCC came the Lowndes County Freedom Organization – later renamed the Black Panthers. On campuses the initially small organization Students for a Democratic Society grew into one of the most significant national anti-war organizations. The biggest marches against the war in Vietnam attracted more than a million people. The tactics were not restricted to marches. For example, three activists, Norman Morrison, Roger La Porte and Alice Herz, publicly set fire to themselves in protest – mirroring the action of the Buddhist monks in Vietnam who had done likewise.

For the most part, the mainstream media backed the US government. There were, however, occasional reports of the effects of US actions. For example, on 6 September 1965, the *New York Times* reported: 'There is a woman who has both arms burned off by napalm and her eyelids so badly burnt that she cannot close them. When it is time for her to sleep, her family put a blanket over her head. The woman had two of her children killed in the airstrike that maimed her.'[3]

The media was, however, not always so frank. When US soldiers massacred as many as 504 people, most of them women, children and old men (and 56 of them babies) in villages in My Lai, on 16 March 1968, it was largely ignored by US news outlets.

It took two months for the news to filter back. The army tried to cover things up. But this attempt was foiled by the action of a soldier named Ron Ridenhour, who circulated a letter recounting events. This was soon accompanied by photos. Two months later, an anti-war news agency in Southeast Asia picked up the story, which was then published in the French press. It was not until a number of the officers involved were put on trial that the US public finally began to take notice. When Lieutenant William Calley was found guilty there was an outcry. Many on the right saw his actions as necessary in the context of the communist threat. Some anti-war campaigners saw him as a scapegoat for the crime of the war itself. Although he was given a life prison sentence, on the instructions of the President he was instead put under house arrest. He was paroled three years later.

The anti-war movement was wise enough not to rely solely on the mainstream media for its Idea Counterpower: it made its own. It is estimated that there were as many as 500 different homemade newspapers – otherwise known as 'zines' – distributed during this period. At least 50 of these were circulated at military bases. They had names such as *Vietnam GI* (Chicago), *Fed Up!* (Washington), *About Face* (Los Angeles) and *Helping Hand* (Idaho). People risked their freedom to smuggle them into the bases and even to the front. And they had an effect.

Some soldiers formed the 'Concerned Officers Movement', who bravely refused to fly certain bombing missions. The resistance was also visible in the military prisons. In 1969 a group of absent-without-leave officers refused to co-operate with prison authorities by sitting down and singing 'We Shall Overcome' at the Presidio Stockade in San Francisco.

Some, however, simply gritted their teeth and kept fighting. One lasting testament is a letter left behind by Keith Franklin, a soldier killed in 1970: 'If you are reading this letter, you will never see me again, the reason being that if you are reading this I have died. The question is whether or not my death has been in vain. The answer is yes. The war that has taken my life and many thousands before me is immoral, unlawful and an atrocity... I had no choice as to my fate. It was predetermined by the war-mongering hypocrites in Washington. As I lie dead, please grant my last request. Help me inform the American people, the silent majority who have not yet voiced their opinions.[4]

Another escalation of Idea Counterpower came with the formation of Vietnam Veterans against the War, a group of returned soldiers who visited every corner of the US, speaking of the horror and injustice of what they had seen. Amongst their number was a future Presidential candidate – John Kerry. There were relatively few people in this group but, when the US removed its troops from Vietnam, 700,000 'less than honorable' discharges were given.[3] This is a quantitative indicator of the breadth of discontent within the US army.

In December 1970, hundreds of former soldiers traveled to Detroit to testify to the atrocities that they had witnessed. The following year more than a thousand former soldiers demonstrated together in Washington against the war. At the climax of the event ex-soldiers approached the fence that surrounds the Capitol building and took turns to throw the medals that they had been awarded over the top.

The government's strategy for recruitment to the army was partly based on idea power: glorifying life with the armed services. It was also based on economic power – attracting poor people in need of a job. The practice of conscription was itself a form of physical power.

Nevertheless, anti-war feeling was strongly felt amongst potential recruits. Universities in particular became hotbeds of anti-war agitation, especially as it was after graduating that young people were expected to sign up. In 1969, 253 student union presidents wrote to the US President to declare their non-cooperation with the draft. By 1972, there were more draft resisters than people signing up to fight.[5]

Music provided another important form of Idea Counterpower. Folk singers Pete Seeger and Joan Baez, for example, were regulars at protest rallies, and during that time they wrote and sang songs – including *We Shall Overcome* – which showed those having doubts about the war that they were not alone. Edwin Starr's *War: What Is It Good For?* went to number one in the charts when it was released in 1970.

When John Lennon arrived in the United States in 1971 he also lent his support to the anti-war movement. Songs such as *Imagine* and *Merry Christmas War is Over* communicated the message to a wider audience. However, his songs were not only to be heard on the radio but also on the streets themselves. *Give Peace a Chance* and *Power to the People* are still sung on demonstrations to this day. The authorities attempted to deport Lennon in 1972. Documents later came to light advising that 'If Lennon's visa was terminated it would be a strategic counter-measure.'[6] Eventually the case received so much publicity that it was dropped, aided by the resignation of Richard Nixon after the Watergate scandal. Through determination and Idea Counterpower, the movement had overcome the state.

But the anti-war movement was not confined to Idea Counterpower. There was significant nonviolent direct action against military recruiters. On one occasion, for example, a group including priests poured blood on draft records, and on another occasion they took them outside and burned them. Actions on university campuses led to the canceling of 40 Reserve Officers Training Corps programs. Physical Counterpower went somewhat further than this. For instance, two campaigners took control of a US ship carrying munitions to Southeast Asia and diverted its course. In another case, activists sabotaged railway links used to carry arms out of a weapons factory.

Some Physical Counterpower went even further. Between 1969 and 1981, the Weather Underground (a group formed by a small number of members of Students for a Democratic Society) threw Molotov cocktails at the house of a judge, planted bombs in police stations, blew up a police statue, blew it up again (after it had been rebuilt), bombed the Pentagon, broke into the FBI (stealing files on leftwing activists) and even succeeded in breaking a person out of prison.[7] Many of them were not imprisoned because the extent to which the police broke the law in searching for them would have to have been revealed in full.

All three kinds of Counterpower were present in the resistance to the war by the African-American community. Black leaders, including Stokely Carmichael,[8] Bobby Seale and (after some delay) Martin Luther King[9] all used their profile to speak out against the Vietnam War. They pointed out what King (in the year before his assassination) called an 'almost facile connection' between the events in Vietnam and the struggles of black people in the US. Although Malcolm X was killed in 1965, he too had spoken out about events in Vietnam – which he compared to the Mau Mau rebellion in Kenya.[10]

One of the members of Malcolm X's organization 'Nation of Islam' was Muhammad Ali – three times world heavyweight boxing champion. He was also an eloquent opposer of the Vietnam War, famously declaring 'I ain't got no quarrel with the Vietcong. No Vietcong ever called me Nigger'. Like many black people, Ali used his Economic Counterpower by refusing to supply his labor as a soldier. When ordered to the military induction center, Ali dramatically refused to stand forward when his name was called. His brave act gave strength and inspiration to many others to do likewise. Although he was accused of being unpatriotic and stripped of his heavyweight title, he won the far greater honor of a place in history.[11]

The immense cost of the Vietnam War correlated with a decrease in funding for anti-poverty programs at home. As social conditions declined, riots in black areas began to break out. Some anti-war campaigners began to claim that the government could soon need to deploy troops in the US itself if the injustice was not stopped.

One anti-war pamphlet explains the escalation of the movement as a whole: 'We have met, discussed, analyzed, lectured, published, lobbied, paraded, sat-in, burned draft cards, stopped troop trains, refused induction, marched, trashed, burned and bombed buildings, destroyed induction centers. Yet the war has gotten steadily worse – for the Vietnamese and, in a very different way, for us'.[12] In line with this, one of the most ambitious protests of all was planned for 1 May 1971 when activists declared that 'if the government won't stop the war, we'll stop the government'. A guide was circulated, detailing road infrastructure in Washington DC that activists could nonviolently block so that government employees could not complete the journey into work. On the day, some barricades were temporarily constructed but the stated goal of the action was foiled – partly because the police knew from the guide exactly where to go. But they could only stop the action by arresting a staggering 14,000 people. In its aim, style and organization (including the use of 'affinity groups') a direct lineage can be traced to the anti-globalization summit protest of Seattle 1999.[13]

The resistance was not confined to the US. For example there were also frequent protests in Europe. In March 1968 this included a notable attempt by the Vietnam Solidarity Campaign to occupy the US embassy in London as the NLF had done (briefly) in Saigon earlier that year. In his 'Autobiography of the 1960s', Tariq Ali describes the scenes first hand. When the protesters overcame a line of police to gain entrance to Grosvenor Square, the horses were brought in: 'A cry went up that "The Cossacks are coming" and an invisible tension united everyone. Arms were linked across the square as the mounted police charged through us to try and break our formation. A hippy who tried to offer a bunch of flowers to a policeman was truncheoned to the ground. Marbles were thrown at the horses and a few policemen but none were surrounded and beaten up... We got close to the imperialist fortress, but by 7pm we decided to evacuate the square. Many comrades were badly hurt and one pregnant woman had been beaten up severely.' For Ali and many other radicals of the time the protest was not only about Vietnam. As he puts it, 'We wanted a new world without wars, oppression and class exploitation, based on comradeship and internationalism.'[14]

In France (the former colonial power in Vietnam) protests

were, if anything, even more wide-ranging in character. The demands spanned from reforms in universities to full-scale revolution – but the call for the US to pull out of Vietnam played a key part. In May 1968, a demonstration involving (amongst others) Daniel Cohn-Bendit was surrounded by police. Given the option to stay or disperse, students and trade unionists occupied the Latin Quarter of Paris and renamed it the 'Heroic Vietnam Quarter'. Barricades were constructed and police attacks were repelled with the cobblestones that people dug up. The slogans of the time live on in legend including 'defend the collective imagination', 'commodities are the opium of the people' and, most famous of all, 'beneath the cobblestones, the beach'. The revolt across Europe prompted a new chant: 'We will fight, we will win, London, Paris, Rome, Berlin.'

As the Counterpower against the war grew both in the US and abroad, so did social permission to break with the authorities. This happened spectacularly in the case of Daniel Ellsberg. Ellsberg was an employee of the RAND Corporation, engaged by the Department of Defense to assist in the collection of internal documents charting government discussions surrounding the war in Vietnam. Following first-hand experience of the war, he realized that he could no longer in good conscience co-operate with the US government. He studiously copied all 7,000 pages of the document he had helped to produce, and then released it to the public. When they were serialized in a major newspaper, they came to be known as 'The Pentagon Papers'.

The release of secret documents such as these helped to further undo the US government's case for war. For example, the government's argument that the war was a battle of liberation on behalf of the Vietnamese people was somewhat undermined by the Pentagon Papers' revelation that 'Only the Viet Cong had any real support and influence on a broad base in the countryside'. The case for the good intent of the US was still further undermined by a memo from the National Security

Council which expressed concern that if the US lost control of Vietnam it could lose control of the entire region, which would be bad because: 'Southeast Asia, particularly Malaya and Indonesia, is the principal world source of natural rubber and tin, and a producer of petroleum and other strategically important commodities'.[3]

The Pentagon Papers also revealed the sensitivity of the administration to public opinion. Initially this led to recommendations that the US should bomb Vietnam so intensely and severely that it would be cowed into submission before the US civil society and press had time to object to what was going on. When this recommendation failed, it was followed by a proposal to destroy locks and dams in order to cause mass starvation without the drama of aerial bombardment. After this, Assistant Secretary of Defense John McNaughton warned the President that: 'There may be a limit beyond which many Americans and much of the world will not permit the United States to go. The picture of the world's greatest superpower killing or seriously injuring 1,000 non-combatants a week, while trying to pound a tiny backward nation into submission, on an issue whose merits are hotly contested, is not a pretty one.'[3]

The first slowing of the war came in 1968, when a request for further troops from the US was declined by the President, who had been advised by the Pentagon that: 'This growing disaffection, accompanied, as it certainly will be, by increased defiance of the draft and growing unrest in the cities because of the belief that we are neglecting domestic problems, runs a great risk of provoking a domestic crisis of unprecedented proportions.'[3]

McGeorge Bundy, a national security adviser to two presidents, concluded that the threat or use of nuclear weapons 'would have totally unacceptable results inside the United States, enraging the opponents of the war and setting general opinion against the new administration with such force as to make it unlikely that the government could ever keep up the American end of the war.'² By the mid-1970s, the US was forced to bring its troops home.

The willingness of campaigners to keep escalating their resistance with Counterpower helped to influence the eventual action of the US government. It came at a cost – the government fought the domestic resistance relentlessly. Nevertheless, the movement was resilient due to a timeless principle: solidarity.

We'll walk hand in hand

The campaign against the war in Vietnam was unprecedented in the US. However, as the movement escalated its tactics, the government escalated its response. Before long, this turned to the use of physical power against the domestic anti-war movement. Interviewed for a documentary released in 2006, a former FBI agent admitted: 'Looking back, it was horrible what we did. We were being used by the government to stop dissent, plain and simple.'⁶

The government's stifling of dissent was felt at large-scale demonstrations. On one occasion the police fired on demonstrators, killing four.¹³ When the government tried to ban demonstrations at the Democratic Convention in Chicago in 1968, people turned up and demonstrated anyway. When the protesters were attacked by police, the images were shown across the country, live on television, as the protesters chanted 'The whole world is watching'. The actions of the police in initiating a riot won greater sympathy for the movement and took attention away from the platitudes of pro-war politicians inside the conference center. Afterwards, eight people were charged with 'intent to incite a riot'. Among them were prominent figures in the anti-war movement, including the radical activists Tom Hayden, Abbie Hoffman and Jerry Rubin, as well as Black Panthers co-founder Bobby Seale. People demonstrated outside their hearings and watched from the gallery. Faced with the Idea Counterpower of their argument in the courtroom, and the support outside it, most of their convictions were dropped on appeal.

In general, black activists faced still greater repression. For example, conscious efforts were made by government to sow seeds of distrust between different black organizations. Bobby Seale was the only one of the 'Chicago Eight' who suffered a long prison sentence following the trial. Deputy Chair Fred Hampton suffered a worse fate.[15] He was killed in bed in his apartment in 1969 by Chicago police. To assist them in their attack, his assassins used a floor-plan supplied by Hampton's 'bodyguard', who was an informant for the FBI. But, as Hampton said during his life, 'you can kill the revolutionary but you can't kill the revolution'. The Panthers maintained their status. Seale even came close to becoming mayor of Oakland in 1973.

Acting army officers who protested were also suppressed. When an army lieutenant simply stood outside the White House with a placard, he was arrested. When two marines spoke to other marines about the immorality of the war they were sentenced to six and ten years respectively. When an army doctor refused to teach 'green beret' soldiers, he was court-martialed and imprisoned. After the nonviolent sit-down protest at the Presidio stockade, the participants were each sentenced to between 14 and 16 years in prison for mutiny. The list goes on. Yet all of these arrestees became *causes célèbres* for the solidarity movement outside prison and only served to increase the Counterpower of the movement. This was especially the case for the Presidio protesters. There was such an outcry in this instance that, when the case was appealed, the charge was downgraded to 'wilful disobedience of a superior officer'. They were released after just 18 months. The power of solidarity helped the movement in its resilience against attack.

Sometimes the state's charges were not even for campaign-related activities. For example, in 1969, police were dispatched to catch radical activist John Sinclair of the White Panthers with a small amount of marijuana. He was sentenced to prison for 10 years, after handing two joints to undercover narcotics officers. However, he was not forgotten. Mass protests and rock concerts were arranged to call for his release. The biggest, a 24-hour concert including John Lennon and Stevie Wonder, had 20,000 attendees, and was broadcast live across the US. Lennon wrote a song for the occasion:

> 'If he'd been a soldier man
> Shooting gooks in Vietnam
> If he was the CIA
> Selling dope and making hay
> He'd be free, they'd let him be
> Breathing air, like you and me
> They gave him ten for two
> What else can the judges do?
> Got to, got to, got to... set him free'

The following Monday, they did. Just three days after the concert, Sinclair was released from prison when the Supreme Court ruled that the state's drugs laws were unconstitutional. The Idea Counterpower of the movement, through their solidarity, had again helped to overwhelm the physical power of the state.

Another celebrated case was that of the nine Catholic campaigners who burned records taken from a draft office and were sentenced to a total of 18 years in prison. Some of the 'Catonsville Nine' succeeded in escaping. One, Mary Moylan, was never found. Another, Daniel Berrigan, was eventually tracked down, but only after a series of daring appearances, including one in front of a large crowd. By escaping, Berrigan and Moylan were in good company. Over the course of the US involvement in Vietnam, thousands of US soldiers deserted. But they could not have done so without the solidarity of people willing to allow the escapees to hide in their homes. Once again, the Counterpower of movement solidarity was able to resist the overweening power of government.

Despite these successes in keeping activists out of prison,

many campaigners and protesters did face time behind bars. For example, the first person to publicly burn his draft card was sentenced to prison for two-and-a-half years. Over the course of the war, 9,000 people were convicted for resisting the draft. However, the sheer numbers of people refusing to fight helped to undermine the government's power – it had neither the economic capacity nor the physical space to sentence and imprison everyone who refused the draft. Over the course of the war more than 200,000 people refused to sign up, yet the government only succeeded in using its physical power of imprisonment against five per cent of them.[5]

Supporters of the war deemed draft resistance to be unpatriotic. Yet the Idea Counterpower of the movement developed to such an extent that draft refusers are remembered in the popular memory not as traitors, but as brave voices for human rights. This was officially recognized in 1977, when many draft resisters were officially 'pardoned' by President Jimmy Carter. This would not have been possible had the mainstream movement opted to condemn the actions of those willing to risk arrest. However, through movement solidarity, and openness to a diversity of tactics, the Idea Counterpower of the anti-war movement won out.

We shall live in peace?

The principles reflected in the song *We Shall Overcome* help to explain why the campaign against the Vietnam War was ultimately successful. The movement escalated to match the power of the government ('We shall overcome'), and used solidarity to stop themselves from being undermined ('We'll walk hand in hand'). The campaign against the war in Vietnam also sheds light on some of the stumbling blocks encountered by the campaigns in the previous chapters. The early climate movement failed to escalate its tactics sufficiently in line with the threat. The peace movement during World War One escalated their tactics to some extent but failed to attract the solidarity necessary to win. Britain's National Union of Mineworkers both escalated their tactics and enjoyed significant solidarity but not on the scale necessary to overcome a government which had been preparing for many years.

Some theoretical weight for the identification of sufficient solidarity and escalation as the key variables is provided by a popular mechanism for analyzing power known as *The Prisoner's Dilemma*. The 'characters' in the game are two people apprehended by the police. As the police do not have enough evidence to convict either party, they separate the arrestees from one another and offer each prisoner two courses of action. They can *defect* (betray the other prisoner with the hope of walking free) or *co-operate* (hope that if both refuse to talk, the police will only be able to prosecute for a minor charge). However, if one person 'defects' and the other 'co-operates' the defector walks free while the co-operator gets a hefty prison sentence.[16]

The model has been much tested and two things have become clear. The first is that the best overall outcome emerges if the arrestees co-operate and resist the temptation to be 'divided and ruled'. However, if one prisoner isn't co-operating, the best strategy is to mirror the actions of the other prisoner. Game theorists call this second strategy 'tit for tat'.[17] Governments have adopted the principles of 'tit for tat' frequently. There are lessons from this when transferred to the politics of Counterpower. The first is that if the government ignores the movement or escalates its tactics, the movement must escalate its tactics also. The second is that the principle and practice of movement solidarity can help provide resilience against attack.

Taken at face value, the 'tit for tat' strategy seems somewhat at odds with Gandhi's observation that 'An eye for an eye makes the whole world blind'. Indeed, one might say that this could quickly lead to avoidable civil wars and the mass suffering which they bring. A closer look, however, reveals that such an approach could actually be in line with Gandhi's philosophy.

The last chapter related political power to the concepts offered by the science of physics. Just as forms of energy can be transformed into one another, so too can forms of political power. A 'tit for tat' strategy does not necessarily mean responding with the same kind of power with which one is attacked. It simply means responding with an equivalent level of power.

In the case of the war in Vietnam, the US government's power to arrest people clearly could not be mirrored by arresting members of the government. However, through applied Idea Counterpower the movement undermined the government, forcing it to backtrack and pardon many of the arrested parties.

But there is another problem with the Prisoner's Dilemma. Equivalent Counterpower responses by the movement could easily lead to stalemate. This is where Gandhi's concept of 'Love Force' comes into its own. Gandhi taught that the opponent's heart could be melted by self-suffering – a view echoed by the argument of Richard Gregg in Chapter 2. The examples so far have shown that Idea Counterpower can help resist the physical power of the state. But Love Force has another benefit. As well as counterbalancing the power of government, it can also lead to a government reconsidering, moving towards the movement, and abandoning its own 'tit for tat' strategy.

This is not to say that every person complicit in causing suffering will be converted simply by the knowledge of the result of their actions. However, every person is a human being with human emotions. Every person also has external pressures brought to bear upon them to do one thing or another. In the context of sufficient Counterpower, people may see the opportunity to pursue a more morally comfortable path. Although conceptions of morality can in themselves be instruments of both power and Counterpower, few human beings can be unaffected by upfront displays of raw humanity.

In the case of the war in Vietnam, RAND employee Daniel Ellsberg was deeply affected when he saw at first hand the suffering to which his work was contributing. Many other soldiers had similar experiences. Without the mass Counterpower movement, it is unlikely that they would have dared to speak out. However, Counterpower did not force them to act as they did – it supported and assisted them to do what they knew, deep down, to be right.

There is another aspect of the learning from this case study that requires further interrogation. A major flaw in game theory as applied to social movements is that there is usually more than one party in the movement. Furthermore there are also usually differences of opinion and approach within the government being targeted. Both of these questions will be looked at further in the following chapter, asking why it was that the movement against apartheid in South Africa eventually ended in success.

1 Chris Brazier, *Vietnam: The Price of Peace*, Oxfam, Oxford, 1992. **2** Kate Hudson, *CND - Now more than ever: The Story of a Peace Movement*, Vision, London, 2005. **3** Howard Zinn, *A People's History of the United States*, Harper & Row, New York, 1980. **4** Letter from Keith Franklin, excerpt online at www.spartacus.schoolnet. co.uk/VNprotest.htm **5** Antiwar and radical history online archive nin.tl/l7uFqV **6** David Leaf & John Schonfeld, *The US vs. John Lennon*, Lions Gate, 2006. **7** Look up the documentary *The Weather Underground*, PBS, 2002 for more on this group. **8** Who is credited with having coined the term 'black power'. **9** As part of the same speech he said 'We as a nation must undergo a radical revolution of values. We must rapidly begin the shift from a "thing-oriented" society to a "person-oriented" society. When machines and computers, profit motives and property rights are considered more important than people, the giant triplets of racism, materialism, and militarism are incapable of being conquered.' The full speech is available online at nin.tl/kQEygW **10** 'African-American involvement in the Vietnam War', nin.tl/n9vQn9 **11** Steve Crawshaw and John Jackson, *Small Acts of Resistance: How Courage, Tenacity and Ingenuity can Change the World*, Union Square, New York, 2010. **12** Undated Mayday Tribe publication, 'May Flowers', quoted in LA Kaufman, 'Ending a War: Inventing a Movement' at nin.tl/l85x0V **13** Kaufman, op cit. **14** Tariq Ali, *Street Fighting Years*, Verso, London, 2005. **15** Noam Chomsky later wrote that Hampton was 'one of the most promising leaders of the Black Panther Party – particularly dangerous because of his opposition to violent acts or rhetoric and his success in community organizing'. **16** Andrew Heywood, *Politics*, Palgrave, London, 2002. **17** Philip Ball, *Critical Mass: How One Thing Leads to Another*, Random House, London, 2002.

5
How apartheid was ended in South Africa

'We can be human only in fellowship, in community, in koinonia, in peace.'

Desmond Tutu

One of the most well-known satires of social-movement organizing comes in the form of a two-minute sketch in the Monty Python film *The Life of Brian*. When the bemused protagonist asks to join the People's Front of Judea they explain that the only people they hate more than the Romans are the Judean People's Front and the Popular Front of Judea. 'What happened to them?' asks another character. 'He's over there,' comes the response. The camera switches to a lone bearded man sitting on the steps. 'Splitter' they all shout. The sketch has been evoked many times since to critique the failure of anti-establishment organizations to unite.

The roll-call of groups that took part in the South African freedom struggle is certainly impressive. Groups opposed to apartheid included the African National Congress, the Pan Africanist Congress, the Congress of South African Trade Unions, the South African Indian Congress, the South African People's Congress, the South African Coloured People's Organization, the National Union of South African Students, the South African Students' Organization, the Congress of South African Students, the South African Youth Congress, the Progressive Party, the Reform Party, the Azanian People's Organization, the South African Communist Party, the Inkatha Freedom Party, the Black Consciousness Movement, the National Forum and the United Democratic Front – and that is to name only some. Within these organizations were many more layers of differences of opinion.

Bitterness between some groups was such that on occasion it led to bloodshed. Yet they collectively succeeded in maintaining sufficient solidarity and applying enough Counterpower to eventually tip the balance. The sheer number of groups and the tensions between some of them make the anti-apartheid struggle a particularly interesting case to look at and ask 'How did they do it?'

As this chapter will show, groups with different approaches can work to complement one another's work, without agreeing on everything. The principles for doing so boil down to three main points. First of all, the groups agreed a shared enemy. Second, they collectively used every kind of Counterpower available to them, escalating over time. Third, they helped one another when under attack by government.

The story of the movement for democracy in South Africa also reveals a new aspect of Counterpower: the fact that the actions of some parts of a movement influence the actions of other parts of it. This could be called 'internal movement Counterpower'.

While the story does not necessarily present a template to follow, it does show us how groups with different interests and different views can ultimately bring about transformational change.

The beginnings of apartheid

In Xhosa and in Zulu, 'Amandla' is the word for power. For decades, it was the rallying cry of the movement for black majority rule, responded to by the cry 'Awethu' – 'to us'. It took decades to achieve their democratic revolution, but eventually South Africans achieved their goal with the use of Counterpower.

During the first half of the 20th century, law after law was passed to discriminate against South Africa's black majority. In 1913 the Land Act took away 87 per cent of the land owned by black people. In 1923 the Urban Areas Act created new slums to provide cheap black labor for white-owned industries. In 1926 the Colour Bar Act prevented black people from practicing skilled trades and in 1936 black Africans were removed from the electoral roll. There was also legislation introduced to discriminate against other non-European groups, including the Asiatic Land Tenure and Indian Representation Act of 1946.

One of the founders of the Natal Indian Congress was Mohandas Gandhi, so it is no surprise that some of the early resistance came from this group, which in 1946 was led by the radical GM Naicker. It organized a campaign of nonviolent passive resistance that saw the Congress' leaders arrested and tried. Signs of increased radicalization of the black community could also be seen, including a strike by African mineworkers over pay and conditions. A year later, the 'Three Doctors Pact' was signed by Dr Naicker of the Natal Indian Congress, Dr Yusuf Dadoo of the Transvaal Indian Congress and Dr Xuma of the ANC. They agreed to campaign together for the full franchise, access to education, housing and land.[1] But it was too late to prevent something terrible taking place the following year.

In 1948, the oppressive United Party, led by Jan Smuts, was defeated by another even more oppressive force – the National Party. The National Party's campaign had been fought using two key slogans, which translate as 'the nigger in his place' and 'the coolies out of the country'. Their programme to deliver it was called *apartheid* – which literally translates as 'apart-hood'.

The new government set about introducing even more discriminatory laws than their predecessors had done. All South

Africans were labeled by color. Mixed marriages were banned, as were sexual relations between blacks and whites. Colored people's limited representation in parliament was revoked. All but the mildest protest against the regime was also outlawed by the 'Suppression of Communism Act', which banned the promulgation of any doctrine that 'promotes political, industrial, social or economic change within the union by the promotion of disturbance or disorder'.

In the years that followed, the new government exploited fears about the 'black peril' of black men having sexual relations with white women, as well as the 'red peril' of concerns about communism. This idea power was supported by media censorship and by the Dutch Reformed Church, which professed to have found a theological foundation for apartheid. Alongside this, the new government had at its command the physical power that came with political control of the coercive organs of the state. This was, of course, buoyed up by economic power, since almost all of the commerce in the country was owned by whites. It was a wall of power that took campaigners almost 50 years to break down. But they did.

Mandela as a young radical

The struggle for democracy in South Africa will always be associated with its figurehead – Nelson Mandela. Mandela spent 27 years in prison before eventually becoming the first black president of his country in 1994. His party was the African National Congress (ANC) – formed to speak up for the rights of black people in South Africa in 1912. Like the early Indian National Congress, it began as a weak, reformist and toothless group committed exclusively to constitutional forms of change. In his autobiography, Mandela reflects that in the early days 'many felt, perhaps unfairly, that the ANC as a whole had become the preserve of a tired, unmilitant, privileged African élite, more concerned with protecting their own rights than those of the masses'.[2] He and others decided to challenge it through the use of internal movement Counterpower.

In 1944, a number of young radicals, including Walter Sisulu, Oliver Tambo and Nelson Mandela, formed the congress Youth League with the intent of 'lighting a fire under the leadership of the ANC'.[3] Following the election of the National Party, the Youth League drew up a program of action to resist the new government's policies. Their proposed tactics against the government included boycotts, strikes and civil disobedience. But their task was not so easy as simply to organize and deliver the actions.

The Youth League sought to establish their approach as the policy of the ANC. The Youth League informed their elders that they would only back candidates for positions within the ANC who supported a more militant approach. They met with the ANC president Dr Xuma and informed him that they would only back him if he adopted a different way of doing things. He refused. In response, the Youth League set about constructing a more radical slate to displace the old guard. At first, however, it was difficult to find 'respectable' candidates to advocate their program. Eventually, Dr Moroka of the Trotskyist-oriented All-African Convention agreed. The Youth League was organized enough, and used enough Idea Counterpower, to install him as ANC President. However, he was later dismissed from the ANC when he opted to disassociate himself from the struggle under cross-examination in court. In his place was elected a leading advocate of nonviolent civil disobedience, and a future winner of the Nobel Peace Prize: Chief Albert Luthuli. By that time the ANC had changed. And it changed because of its first oppositional campaign of defiance.

In late 1951 the ANC's annual conference endorsed the sending of a letter to Prime Minister Dr Malan. It was not a pleading letter, like those sent in times gone by. This time it was a set of demands. The missive noted that the ANC had attempted every means of constitutional engagement to no avail. It warned that if the six most discriminatory laws were not repealed by 12 February 1952, a campaign of mass civil disobedience would be instigated. It received a curt reply which stated that whites have a right to separateness and that law breakers would be treated as criminals.

Four months later the campaign began. The plan was very simple: to ignore the segregation laws that had been introduced. Black people would enter whites-only parts of town without the relevant documentation, would sit in whites-only sections of public transport, and walk the streets after curfew. With the range of segregated areas, there was no end of opportunities to resist.

The Defiance Campaign was an important change of gear for the ANC. Even on the first day of the campaign, 250 people were arrested for breaking unjust laws. Over the course of the whole campaign, 8,500 people followed suit. In the context of the style of campaigns up to that point, this was a significant number. Yet in the context of a country of 20 million people, it amounted more to targeted defiance than to destabilizing mass action. The planned second wave, involving strikes and other mass actions, was never reached.

The government used the Suppression of Communism Act to stifle movement organizers. One tactic used was 'banning'. Strict orders were placed upon campaigners, prohibiting attendance at gatherings or membership of certain organizations. The Minister of Justice could impose these at will, without the accused person being charged or tried. The state also dispatched undercover police officers and *agents provocateurs* to inform on and attempt to discredit the movement. They made mass arrests and in 1953 the South African parliament approved detention without trial for those involved in such campaigns.

The campaign did not win the repeal of the six unjust laws; its organizers did not expect that it would. The campaign did, however, succeed in building the skills of activists and organizers, who had never engaged in resistance on such a scale before. As a result, more civil disobedience took place, for example in opposition to the eviction of black people from the township of Sophiatown in 1955. Most importantly, the defiance campaign also transformed the ANC, whose membership increased fivefold, from 20,000 to 100,000.[4] It was a triumph of internal movement Counterpower for the young radicals of the Youth League.

In the wake of the Defiance Campaign, a white liberal named Helen Suzman was elected to parliament. There, she was a lonely parliamentary voice against the apartheid regime for the following 36 years. She suffered opprobrium for her efforts, and was forced to endure harassment by the security forces and anti-Semitic abuse, but she successfully used her position to investigate and highlight human rights abuses in the country.

Another important outcome of the Defiance Campaign was the relationships built between different groups, of the sort that are best forged in the face of adversity. The campaign was co-ordinated by a 'Joint Planning Council', which also included representatives of other Congresses. With trust built, this gave way to a 'National Consultative Council', which included the South African Indian Congress, Coloured People's Congress, South African Congress of Trade Unions and the Congress of Democrats. The last of these groups was another direct outcome of the Defiance Campaign – a coming together of white people sympathetic to the freedom struggle, formed on the initiative of the ANC. The Congress of Democrats included but was not dominated by white members of the banned South African Communist Party.

The Defiance Campaign brought in more supporters, many of whom were willing to go further for the cause than ever before. The movement also won its first friend in Parliament and new allies amongst the white community. The balance was slowly beginning to change. But it would take a long time yet before it would tip in the movement's favor.

The Freedom Charter

In 1955 the largest representative assembly that South
Africa had ever seen was called by the ANC and its allies. It
was named the Congress of the People and was attended
by 3,000 South Africans. For months beforehand activists
had traveled the country collecting 'freedom demands' from
ordinary people. These were then compiled and edited into a
single document – the Freedom Charter. The Charter was
summed up by its first demand: 'The People Shall Govern!'
Like the Three Doctors Pact before it, the document was not
only a call for a non-racial electoral system but for the material
conditions of freedom. It called for 'free and compulsory
education', 'living wages and shorter hours of work' and 'land
to be given to all landless people'.[5] The document represented
a new level of Idea Counterpower, and a new level of agreement
between the Congresses, from the leadership to the grassroots.

The Idea Counterpower generated made the authorities
nervous. On its second day, the Congress of the People was
dispersed by South African police. By then, though, the charter
had been read and approved. Worried about the growing
Counterpower being utilized against it, the government also
moved to the next level. In December 1956, 156 movement
leaders were arrested. Amongst them were Nelson Mandela,
ANC president Chief Luthuli, South African Indian Congress
leader Yusuf Dadoo, Albertina and Walter Sisulu, and the
Communist Ruth First. Also in the dock was Ruth First's
husband Joe Slovo – an activist and theoretician whose writings
shed light on the inner workings of the anti-apartheid campaign's
strategy to this day. The charge against them was high treason.
The trial dragged out over the following four years.[6]

The evidence was frequently odd – for example some labels
denoting vegetarian and non-vegetarian food were produced.
Much of the evidence was based on an 'expert' witness – a
political science professor named Andrew Murray who declared
that the Freedom Charter was 'communistic' in character. In

response, defense lawyer Vernon Berrange read out a series of statements to Andrew Murray and invited him to comment on whether they were 'communistic' or not. Murray found himself labeling statements by Abraham Lincoln, Woodrow Wilson and former South African President Dr Malan as such. Eventually, Dr Murray even labeled as 'communistic' a statement that he had made himself!

The state found ways to cause its opponents the maximum economic hardship. The defendants could not work while they were sitting in court, and some lost their jobs altogether. Some managed to scrape by. Then, in 1958, the state worsened matters by moving the trial from Johannesburg to Pretoria. The new location required a five-hour daily round trip for the defendants at considerable expense – in time as well as money.

The stress of the trial, the effort of the commute, and the attempt to maintain even basic work and contact with family was physically and emotionally grinding for the defendants. The state had found yet another way of using physical power to try to crush those who dared to oppose it.

On 29 March 1961, Judge Rumpff found Mandela and his colleagues not guilty. They celebrated – but not for long. A series of events during the Treason Trial had served to change the movement and to persuade it to try a new kind of resistance.

The movement splits

The Freedom Charter had caused consternation amongst some in the ANC. Africanists rejected all co-operation with white groups while the 'Charterists' promoted maximum co-operation with others in pursuit of the demands in the Freedom Charter. As the conflict looked increasingly irresolvable, some former ANC Youth League members decided to set up their own organization – the Pan Africanist Congress (PAC). They regarded it as even more radical and militant than the organization they had left. They advocated a socialist united states of Africa but abhorred the white-led Communist Party.

Robert Sobukwe of the PAC and Nelson Mandela of the ANC were old colleagues, but with the new organizations came new tensions. Mandela recalls: 'We welcomed anyone brought into the struggle by the PAC', but qualifies this with the claim that 'the role of the organization was almost always that of a spoiler. They would ask people to go to work when we called for a general strike and make misleading statements to counter any pronouncement we would make. Yet the PAC aroused hope in me that although the founders were former ANC men, unity between our two groups would be possible.'[2] Unity may have been possible in theory, but in practice it proved elusive.

In 1959 the ANC Congress decided to plan for a mass campaign against the requirement for non-white people to carry a pass stating their exact racial group. The PAC opted not to work with the ANC but to launch its own anti-pass campaign 10 days before that of the ANC was due to begin. They then invited the ANC to join the PAC campaign. The ANC refused.

Against this background, the PAC entered the spotlight of the world. On 21 March 1960 Robert Sobukwe and others in the PAC executive marched to Orlando police station in Soweto in protest at the pass laws. They carried no pass, and turned themselves in for arrest. Their call was for such actions to be repeated across the country. In many places the call was taken up. In Cape Town the biggest anti-pass protests that the city had ever seen took place. But it was the protests in Sharpeville – a township 35 miles south of Johannesburg – that went down in history.

As in Orlando, a group several thousand strong approached the police station, without their passes. The demonstrators were unarmed and peaceful. The police were not. Without warning, the police began to shoot. As the crowd ran, the police continued to shoot: 69 people were killed, most of them shot in the back. The massacre made the front pages of newspapers all over the world. This was soon followed by protests all around the world. Seeing the need to recognize what had happened, the ANC abandoned its previous plans and organized mass demonstrations of mourning in solidarity with those killed. On 26 March, ANC president Chief Luthuli burned his pass. On 28 March, Mandela burned his, alongside thousands of other South Africans. The government responded by declaring a state of emergency, and imposing martial law. Already on bail, Mandela was once more thrown in prison. Both the ANC and the PAC were banned. Although the state of emergency was eventually lifted, the ANC and PAC remained banned organizations until 1990. The movement was forced to find new ways of operating.

It was in this context that conversations began to take place about how the struggle might continue now that even membership of the main anti-apartheid groups was a crime. In the months following the trial for treason, an all-night secret meeting took place between the different congresses to hammer out a difficult question – should the movement against apartheid now turn to armed struggle?

Advocates of nonviolence, including Chief Luthuli, saw peaceful (if illegal) protest as a principle that could not be violated. In this he was supported by many others in the movement, especially many from the South African Indian Congress for whom Gandhi was an ongoing inspiration. One campaigner in particular argued eloquently that nonviolence had not failed the movement, but the movement had failed nonviolence.

Mandela did not share this view. He argued that nonviolence was a tactic that should be abandoned when it no longer worked, that it was immoral to offer people no response to attacks by the state and that, as violence was already breaking out, it would be better if it were directed by an organized force. After arguing through the night, his position won out.

Mandela was authorized to set up an autonomous body that would plan a campaign of organized violence against the state. The organization came to be known as 'MK' – short for

'Umkhonto We Sizwe', which translates into English as 'Spear of the Nation'. Walter Sisulu and Joe Slovo were among the first recruits to the high command.

The central plank of Umkhonto strategy was a five-page document entitled Operation Mayibuye. It carefully laid out the power of the movement and the power of the state, identifying weak spots in the state machinery that they could 'shamelessly attack'. First and foremost, the plan called for Economic Counterpower – a complete enforcement of an international boycott and for the international trade union movement to refuse to handle weapons destined for the South African government. Following this, it proposed Idea Counterpower through leaflet drops from planes and daily radio transmissions. The ground prepared, there would follow a campaign of bombings against strategic transport links, power stations, security forces and people they termed 'irredeemable government stooges'. This would form the precursor for a guerrilla war of liberation, led by troops armed and trained abroad.[7] Only after the bombing attacks had begun did armed struggle become the official policy of the ANC.

The government's top priority became to capture the high command of Umkhonto we Sizwe, and especially its highest commander – Nelson Mandela. On 5 August 1962, they got their man. On 11 July 1963 they found the evidence against him: the Operation Mayibuye document.

This time there was little doubt as to whether the defendants had broken the law. But still there was scope for building Idea Counterpower in the courtroom as the defendants sought to 'put the state on trial'. Speaking for the gallery, the reporters and the people in generations to come who would find inspiration in his words, Mandela finished his address from the witness box with some immortal words: 'During my lifetime I have dedicated my life to this struggle of the African People. I have fought against white domination and I have fought against black domination. I have cherished the ideal of a democratic and free society in which all persons live together in harmony and with equal opportunities. It is an ideal which I hope to live for and to achieve. But if needs be, it is an ideal for which I am prepared to die'.[8] In the end, Mandela did not face death, but life – in prison.

Now a banned organization, committed to the inherently hierarchical and secretive tactics of armed struggle, the ANC was no longer the mass participation organization of just a few years earlier. The leaders of both the ANC and PAC were undercover, abroad or in prison. Once again, the scales weighed heavily against them. But it was not the end for the freedom struggle.

Black Consciousness and Biko

Although the guerrilla uprising planned in the Operation Mayibuye document never happened (at least not on a national scale), some aspects were implemented, including Economic Counterpower. Some years earlier, Luthuli had called on South African exiles in Britain (South Africa's biggest foreign investor) to begin a boycott campaign of South African goods. In the wake of the Sharpeville Massacre, this organization broadened its focus and named itself the Anti-Apartheid Movement, although its primary Counterpower tactic remained the economic boycott. In the end it would be a key ingredient in bringing the regime down. From the 1960s right through to the 1990s, the international boycott of South African goods grew across the world.

The international boycott also used Idea Counterpower. This was especially the case with the sporting boycott. South Africa was expelled from FIFA (the body governing world football) in 1964 and from the International Olympic Committee in 1970 after proposing all-white teams. When South African sporting teams did tour they were frequently disrupted by pitch invasions. Keenly watched by white South Africans, this helped to emphasize that the rest of the world found apartheid unacceptable. News of the protests reached political prisoners when their white guards complained about the disruptions to their favorite sports. This way the prisoners, starved of newspapers, knew that their cause had not been forgotten. In a similar, and highly significant, act of Idea Counterpower, the World Alliance of Reformed Churches expelled the Dutch Reformed Church in the 1980s.

Meanwhile, the harsh policies of the apartheid regime did not let up. The government sought to remove black people from the cities. Black people were banned from constructing buildings or establishing businesses in urban areas. Government instructions issued in 1967 declared 'No stone is to be left unturned to achieve the settlement in the homelands of non-productive Bantu at present residing in the European areas.'9 The missive defined 'non-productive' people as 'the aged, the unfit, widows and women with dependent children'. The government also took steps to keep living conditions for black people low. By 1970, the average number living in what was known as a 'matchbox' house in Soweto was 13. According to the Associated Chambers of Commerce, the average wage for a black person working in industry was 30 per cent below what would be necessary to provide for a family of five in Soweto.9 Black people were banned from striking or even having membership of a trade union.

A new wave of militant energy now emerged, organized around material grievances, from the grassroots up. Resistance to rent hikes and evictions grew. There were rent strikes, pickets, demonstrations, and even an instance where communities brought buckets of excrement to the offices of local decision-makers so that they could experience the smell for themselves.

A catalyst in this new wave of revolt was a black medical student named Steven Biko. Organizing independently of political parties, he added a new ingredient to the struggle – a new form of Idea Counterpower that he called Black Consciousness. Claiming that 'the most potent weapon of the oppressor is the mind of the oppressed', Biko argued that in order for black

South Africans to liberate themselves physically they must first liberate themselves psychologically. In 1970, Biko wrote in a student newsletter that 'the type of black man we have today has lost his manhood. Reduced to an obliging shell, he looks with awe at the white power structure and accepts what he regards as the inevitable position'.[9] To correct this, he set about celebrating pride in black achievements and promoting the capability of black people to act for themselves without the support of well-meaning white liberals. One of his most popular sayings was: 'Black man, you are on your own.'

The regime used idea power against Biko by demonizing him in the white-owned media. They also used physical power. In 1973, Biko was banned from speaking in public, from writing for, or being quoted in, any publication, and from being with more than one person at a time. He was harassed constantly, and was arrested more than 20 times. The last time was in August 1977, when he broke his banning orders to attend a meeting in Cape Town. For 20 days he was kept naked in solitary confinement. He was then beaten and interrogated, still naked, wearing leg irons and handcuffs, before being transferred 700 miles to a prison hospital. He died from his injuries. When news of his death emerged, the authorities initially claimed that it was due to a hunger strike. It was a white liberal newspaper editor who uncovered the truth of Biko's death. Despite their differences, co-operation between quite different strands of the resistance movement stopped one of the great crimes of the apartheid government from being covered up.[10]

Even in Biko's lifetime though, he saw the effects of his ideas. In Soweto, school students began to refuse to be taught in Afrikaans, which they considered to be the language of their oppressors. They boycotted classes, then organized school strikes, then took to the streets. It was on one such occasion, on 16 June 1976, that the regime responded with new heights of brutality. As the students marched, holding banners and singing songs, the police shot and killed a 13-year-old boy. The killing sparked a wave of revolt across Soweto. In the end 600 lay dead and 4,000 wounded. Many of them were schoolchildren.[11]

The Soweto uprising put South Africa on front pages across the world once again. Any justification that the regime put forward lacked credibility placed next to pictures of South African soldiers shooting schoolchildren. This in turn helped weaken the regime's economic power as sanctions were imposed, companies concerned about instability thought twice about investing in the country, and others experienced renewed calls upon them by their European and American customers to pull out. The regime's physical power was weakened by a UN arms embargo imposed in 1977.

Although organized independently of any political party, one effect of the uprising was to bring many radicalized new recruits to the ANC's armed struggle. Following events in Soweto, many young people left South Africa for neighboring countries. There they joined with members of Umkhonto We Sizwe to learn the methods of guerrilla warfare. From 1977, Umkhonto We Sizwe escalated its operations in South Africa, targeting police stations, government offices, fuel storage tanks and a military base.

In 1980, a Soweto newspaper began a campaign with a banner headline reading 'Free Mandela'. Although many people did not know who Mandela was (he quips in his autobiography that some people thought his first name was 'Free'), he became an icon for the campaign. This soon spread across the world as roads, buildings, student unions and rooms were named after him to ensure that his name was not forgotten.

Throughout the freedom struggle, songs were an important tool of Idea Counterpower, reinforcing collective identity. For example, *Nkosi Sikelel'i Afrika* (later to become the national anthem) was regularly sung at rallies and at funerals. Another popular song was *Senzeni Na?* – a call-and-response lament asking 'What have we done?' with the reply 'Our only crime is being Black'.[12] In the 1980s, the music went global. 'Free Nelson Mandela' by the Special AKA and Peter Gabriel's song 'Biko' were just two in a slew of songs composed and played at packed stadiums, benefit concerts and rallies across the world.

Slowly but surely, the apartheid regime began to make piecemeal reforms, recognizing, in the words of Prime Minister PW Botha, that 'we must adapt otherwise we shall die'.[9] Education was improved for blacks (although still kept separate), the laws on inter-racial marriage were relaxed and, following a swathe of unofficial labor disputes, Africans were finally permitted to join trade unions. A new culture of militancy was rising. But the movement hadn't finished yet.

Tipping the balance

One of the piecemeal reforms introduced by Prime Minister PW Botha was a new electoral arrangement designed to divide and rule the resistance, giving some groups preference over others. He proposed a new 'tricameral' parliamentary system through which white people, 'coloreds' (people of mixed race) and Indians would have separate chambers. Meanwhile, black people had local authorities seen by many as a substitute for black representation in the national parliament and as a way of legitimizing apartheid.

It was during an unplanned part of a speech by the cleric Allan Boesak that a proposal was made to form a front to oppose the new structures. It received a phenomenal response. A committee was immediately set up to look into this. Just three weeks later, a new alliance was put together – the United Democratic Front. In time it would include 500 groups in its membership, who managed to temporarily put their differences aside. These included community campaign groups of every race, Communists and underground members of the ANC. Many black African churches were also very much involved and Bishop (later Archbishop) Desmond Tutu became a well-known figurehead. Early in the UDF's existence it adopted the Freedom Charter as its statement of principles. Their slogan was 'UDF unites; apartheid divides'.[13]

However, the UDF did not unite every activist in South Africa. In some ways echoing the debates between the Charterists and the Africanists in times gone by, a parallel front called the National Forum was established. The UDF was perceived by many as the unofficial face of the ANC in the country while the National Forum was formed out of the institutions of the Black Consciousness Movement, suspicious of the UDF's co-operation with white opponents of apartheid. Although the rivalries were real and on occasion aggressive, there were also important similarities between the two coalitions. Both opposed economic oppression as well as racial oppression. Across the movement, study groups discussed the possibilities of 'socialism from below'. And there were some groups that neither front would work with. Any organization that broke the sporting boycott or which worked with the government was seen as part of the institution the Fronts were challenging and was refused membership.

The first task was to resist the legitimization of the new parliaments. In the event, less than 20 per cent of those eligible to vote in the 1983 election did so – a great success for the movement. The next action of the UDF was to attempt to collect a million signatures against apartheid. It only achieved about a third of that target but the campaign made the Front both better known and bigger. The government responded by arresting a number of leading figures in the UDF under suspicion of treason. Their evidence rested on the singing of freedom songs and the making of speeches attacking the government. The case eventually collapsed, but only after taking the campaigners out of action for some time.

The movement was getting ready to become more confrontational. In 1985 the time arrived. Over the course of that year, 8,000 anti-apartheid campaigners were arrested. One of them was a community organizer named Mkhuseli Jack who, in July 1985, announced a consumer boycott of white-owned businesses. The announcement was made at a funeral – the only kind of public gathering still allowed. The following Monday, Port Elizabeth was all but empty. The government replied by calling a state of emergency and giving soldiers arbitrary stop and search powers. Activists added further demands: the freeing of political prisoners and an end to the state of emergency. Jack was arrested, along with other boycott leaders, but the boycott continued until white businesses agreed to lobby for black leaders to be released. When Jack was released but placed under house arrest, he tore up his banning orders in front of a mass rally.[14]

Later the same year, Allan Boesak planned a nonviolent march to Pollsmoor Prison, where Mandela, Sisulu and others were being held. When the security forces sought to intercept the march, 28 people were killed. In the months that followed, there were riots in townships across South Africa. In Natal, members of the Inkatha Freedom Party and the UDF began to fight with one another. In other areas there was violence between black and Indian groups.

In 1986 a shift in tactics took place from 'ungovernability' to 'people's power' as some local communities declared themselves autonomous. According to a press statement from the time: 'The seeds of people's power are beginning to germinate and spread their roots. People's committees, street committees and comrades' committees are emerging on a growing scale as popular organs in place of the collapsed racist stooge administrations. People's courts, people's defense militia and other popular organs of justice are, in many cases, challenging the legitimacy of the racists' machinery of justice and their uniformed forces of repression.'[15] According to a trade unionist quoted in the *New Internationalist* that year, the action raised the level of consciousness amongst the country's working people, as it 'instilled an understanding of the kind of order we want, instilled in people a confidence that they have the capacity to run their own society'. Mass strikes followed, organized by the Congress of South African

Trade Unions (COSATU) – an explicitly anti-apartheid trade union alliance formed the previous year.

As the movement grew it began to speak of something even bigger. Along with COSATU the Mass Democratic Movement was launched in 1989. It called another Defiance Campaign (mirroring the activities of 1952). Public events were held which unilaterally declared facilities open to all, irrespective of color. Black patients then turned up at white hospitals and demanded to be treated. Organized groups of people of different races took to segregated beaches and buses to show that, if the government would not repeal unjust laws, the people would simply disregard them.

The growing protests gave a higher profile to South Africa on the international stage, which in turn gave a boost to the international boycott movement. A particularly successful part of this was the boycott of Barclays Bank. In Britain, this was so widespread that Barclays' share of the student bank-account market dropped from 27 per cent to 15 per cent.[16] Barclays was forced to withdraw from the country in a high-profile and embarrassing climb-down. Meanwhile, demonstrations grew for sanctions by governments against South Africa.

Meanwhile, since the 1970s, the countries surrounding South Africa had one by one changed from white regimes sympathetic to the National Party to black-led regimes, sympathetic to the left-wing programs of the ANC and PAC. The ANC's relationship with the South African Communist Party helped secure training and weapons from the newly Soviet-aligned states while the PAC – who had also turned to armed struggle – operated from bases in Zimbabwe. Anti-apartheid troops were stationed just over the border from South Africa on many sides and a number of attacks on infrastructure within the country took place.

Every part of the anti-apartheid resistance adopted different tactics. MK and the PAC threatened the Physical Counterpower of armed revolution. The UDF and National Forum used the Economic Counterpower, Physical Counterpower and Idea Counterpower offered by the tactic of civil disobedience. The Idea Counterpower of the international sporting boycott and the Economic Counterpower of the sanctions and product-boycotts weakened the regime still more. Not everyone agreed with all of the tactics used. Nevertheless, a way was eventually found for disparate groups to work together and weaken the regime.

Perhaps sensing the changing balance of power, Mandela engaged in an action that he knew would be controversial. In 1985, while in solitary confinement and unable to consult with his colleagues, he contacted the government and offered to open talks. The regime initially ignored his approaches. But as the movement's Counterpower continued to grow, the government accepted the offer. Over a series of conversations, Mandela impressed his opponents, persuaded them that he was someone with whom they could work, and in so doing began slowly to entice the government away from its extremist stance.

As the Cold War neared its end, the idea power of the regime was weakened still more. No longer could they explain away their unacceptable policies to the rest of the world by claiming that their apartheid system was a necessary bulwark against communist insurgents. As a result, South Africa's flow of economic support from anti-communist countries receded.

In the end, the combination of Physical Counterpower, Economic Counterpower and Idea Counterpower was enough to create a deadlock. Mandela broke the deadlock by negotiating with his opponent. South Africa was, at long last, free from white minority rule.

Unity is strength?

Many an organization has proclaimed on its banners that 'Unity is Strength'. Unity could be defined as 'singleness', 'harmony' or 'being in accord'. Singleness was certainly not a factor in South Africa's freedom struggle. Neither was harmony. However, some level of agreement between different groups was an important factor in the success of the movement. In the first major alliance of the anti-apartheid campaign – the Congress Alliance – the ANC was the biggest group. However, in the interest of the collective power of the movement, it opted to be just one vote among five. The second major alliance was the UDF, the size of which allowed it to deliver on the strategies of ungovernability and people's power.

Probably the most controversial alliance in the freedom struggle was the working agreement between the ANC and the South African Communist Party. But despite the best efforts of the government, the ANC and the SACP refused to be divided and ruled. As a young man, Mandela had sponsored a motion to expel all members of the Communist Party from the ANC. Gradually, though, he amended his view, through friendships with Communist activists and readings of Marxist literature. In his autobiography he writes: 'dialectical materialism seemed to offer both a searchlight highlighting the dark night of racial oppression and a tool that could be used to end it... African nationalists and African communists generally had far more to unite them than to divide them.'[2]

There were also significant differences between the Congress Alliance and the UDF. The Congress Alliance was ultimately a top-down organization, instigated and dominated by educated élites which debated, devised and delivered campaigns for their supporters. When the leaders were removed, the popular movement subsided. In contrast, the UDF was formed in direct response to grassroots militant energy. The National Executive Council *did* develop campaigns but the alliance was so large that the grassroots did not rely upon its direction. Thus, when leaders and organizers were taken out of action by the authorities, the action continued.

Those at the top of hierarchical organizations often seem to have the belief that 'unity' means agreeing with whatever the leader says. But disunity in political organizations is both natural and necessary. In 1948, for example, when the ANC leadership refused to countenance the idea of embracing civil disobedience, the Youth League saw fit to oust the old guard and replace them with more radical figures. This would not have been possible if they had followed the policy of 'unity at all costs'.

Sometimes disagreements can be resolved differently. For example, despite fundamental differences over the establishment of an armed force, people in the movement with different viewpoints found a way to work with each other. Chief Luthuli focused on the promotion of the international boycott, while Mandela, Slovo and Sisulu turned their attention to military preparations through MK. This uneasy alliance continued after the banning of the ANC. The UDF, for example, stated its commitment to nonviolent methods, but also had an understanding with the ANC. These kinds of differences are easier to sustain in the context of a number of organizations than within a single organization.

The setting up of breakaway groups is necessary if conflicts within organizations have been unresolved for so long that all-important energy is being diverted from the cause and towards internal grievances. This was what Robert Sobukwe and others did when they established the PAC. Of course this can (and did) lead to arguments continuing as disagreements between organizations. Nevertheless, the PAC brought new people to the struggle as a whole who were attracted by its radical Africanist approach and who were uncomfortable with the compromises made in the Congress Alliance.

There is a case to be made that the very hierarchical nature of the ANC and PAC actually contributed to the disunity of the movement – as acrimony between the respective leaderships translated to acrimony between respective supporters. The banning of both organizations and the imprisonment of their leaders may have forced grassroots activists from both groups to find ways of working with one another.

Another question to consider in the context of the anti-apartheid struggle is the respective roles played by 'insider' and 'outsider' forces. For example, there was recognition of the good work of the MP Helen Suzman, but also recognition that constitutional methods could not bring about the transformational change desired. Her most important contribution was to strengthen the hand of the extra-parliamentary movement, rather than the movement strengthening her hand in parliament.

Some people who might have claimed to be exerting 'insider' pressure were the black councilors. Yet they were rejected outright by the movement as puppets of the regime and themselves became the targets of protest. Alliance building may have helped, but it was not unconditional.[17]

Ultimately though, 'insider' pressure did help tip the balance when Mandela began negotiations with government. So if 'insider' pressure was eventually so important, was the movement wrong to engage in oppositional tactics for so long? The evidence suggests that even had the movement wanted to open talks earlier, the regime would have refused – as they did with Mandela's first approaches. Furthermore, for the decades that the ANC restricted itself to constitutional tactics, it was consistently sidelined, even under the comparatively benign administrations before the National Party came to power.

Over 40 years, the movement built sufficient Counterpower to be able to enter talks as an equal partner. Only then were negotiations likely to be fruitful. The very fact that a man serving a life prison sentence would eventually exert 'insider' pressure on the President of South Africa is testament to the Counterpower of the anti-apartheid movement at home and abroad.

What happened at those negotiations is also important. In the end Gandhi's argument that 'self-suffering' has the capacity to transmute the oppressor was a factor in tipping the balance. Mandela's self-suffering and continued resolve helped to break the deadlock and liberate his country from apartheid. A 'Rainbow Alliance' was then established to oversee the largely peaceful transition to full elections.

The question of whether and how South Africa could achieve full liberation from both racial and economic oppression was hotly discussed throughout the movement's history – especially in the later years. For example in 1976, Joe Slovo warned that 'If every racist statute were to be repealed tomorrow, leaving the economic status quo undisturbed, "white domination" in its most essential aspects would remain... There can be no halfway house unless the national struggle is stopped in its tracks and is satisfied with the co-option of a small black élite into the presently forbidden areas of economic and political power.'[18] It would seem that the warning was not heeded.

According to the historian Martin Meredith, the white community came to accept the adage 'give them parliament and keep the banks'.[9] The social-democratic principles of the Freedom Charter as reflected in the 'Redistribution and Development Plan' were abandoned in favor of the neoliberal policies associated with the World Bank and IMF. As a result, South Africa remains, at the time of writing, one of the most unequal countries in the world. Many campaigners today argue that, while the visual characteristics of apartheid are receding, the economic impacts remain, or are even getting worse. But the struggle against the new (economic) apartheid in South Africa is still very much alive, as South Africans continue to take to the streets. Their call and response chant is frequently the same as in times gone by: 'Amandla!' (power), 'Awethu!' (to us). [19]

1 Full text available on the website of the Gandhi-Luthuli Documentation Centre at nin.tl/kVkCEI **2** Nelson Mandela, *Long Walk to Freedom*, Abacus, London, 1994. **3** Though less well known, Peter Mda and Anton Lembede were the key movers in establishing the ANCYL. **4** Some estimates suggest that ANC membership was more like 5,000 before the Defiance Campaign. **5** The full text of the Freedom Charter can be found at nin.tl/lwWGC2 **6** A full account is included in Mandela's *Long Walk to Freedom*, op cit. **7** The full Operation Mayibuye document is available at the O'Malley online archive nin.tl/knSipp **8** The full speech is included in Great Speeches of the 20th Century, Random House, London, 2008. **9** Martin Meredith, *The State of Africa*. Free Press, London, 2005. **10** Donald Woods, *Biko*, Penguin, London, 1976. **11** A first-hand account is available in Denis Herbstein, *White Man, We Want to Talk to You*, Pelican, London, 1978. **12** For a beautiful documentary about this, watch *Amandla: A Revolution in Four Part Harmony*, 2002. **13** There is a picture of a t-shirt bearing this slogan on the South Africa History online website at nin.tl/iYXyyO **14** Peter Ackerman and Jack DuVall, *A Force More Powerful: A*

Century of Nonviolent Conflict, St Martin's Press, New York, 2000. **15** ANC Press statement, 'From Ungovernability to People's Power', nin.tl/qlVSQD **16** Steve Crawshaw and John Jackson, *Small Acts of Resistance: How Courage, Tenacity and Ingenuity can Change the World*, Union Square, New York, 2010. **17** Campaigners in the global justice movement debating whether to work with corporate-backed 'astro-turf' organizations might take note. **18** Joe Slovo et al, *Southern Africa: The New Politics of Revolution*, Penguin, London, 1976. **19** Trevor Ngwane and Patrick Bond in Abramsky (ed), *Sparking a World-wide Energy Revolution – Social Struggles in the Transition to a Post-Petrol World*, AK Press, Oakland, 2009

6
How the vote was won in Britain

'The idea of hereditary legislators is as inconsistent as that of hereditary judges or hereditary juries; and as absurd as a hereditary mathematician, or a hereditary wise man.'

Tom Paine

According to the scriptwriting guru Robert McKee, a good screenplay begins with a few characters facing a problem. The tension picks up as they try to do something about it, learning and meeting new characters along the way and facing new complications. Then a crisis point is reached when the characters have to use what they have learned to challenge their foe. Eventually the story resolves with victory or loss for the protagonist.[1] To me that sounds rather like a campaign. Perhaps that is why there are so many good films about campaigners.

In the course of researching this book, I read a number of theories proposed by different writers about the stages of successful campaigns.[2] Many of them seemed to resonate with one another and with the histories and autobiographies I was reading. But the one that was most applicable was not a theory in the traditional sense, but the famous maxim already examined: 'First they ignore you, then they laugh at you, then they fight you, then you win.'

It is an inspiring quotation but it is not without its problems – one of which is the implied inevitability. The other problem is that it can be inferred that the process of change is quite passive. It isn't. But from what I can gather, if movements respond to each of these strategies of élites one by one, the maxim is a useful guide to action. When they ignore you, successful movements respond by raising the consciousness of the masses. When they laugh at you, the protest movement co-ordinates to show its strength. When they fight you, the movement confronts in return, to a similar degree, while at the same time continuing to raise consciousness and co-ordinating. And when you win, the movement does what it can to consolidate gains to prevent their slipping away again. Briefly put:

Consciousness is the stage of realizing that there is a problem and creating the conditions for Counterpower.

Co-ordination is the stage of building Counterpower through a movement to challenge the problem.

Confrontation is the stage when Counterpower is used most intensely, as the movement challenges the target's power outright.

Consolidation is about maintaining Counterpower, adjusting to the new balance of power following the Confrontation Stage, and ensuring that it turns into real-life change.

This is not an exact science. To quote Joe Slovo: 'Every political struggle has specific phases and stages... but there is no Chinese wall between these stages; they flow from and into one another'.[3] This is echoed by the US community organizer Bill Moyer, who writes in reference to his eight-stage model that 'from past experience, real-life social movements will neither fit exactly nor move through the stages linearly, smoothly, or in the manner outlined'.[4]

'Stages' models can, however, be of practical use. In

presentations to activist groups, Moyer would point out that 'Every major social movement of the last 20 years has undergone significant collapse, in which activists believed their movements had failed, the power institutions were too powerful, and their own efforts were futile'. He discovered that presenting a stages model 'usually lifted morale, helped activists recognize their movement's successes, restored energy, and helped develop strategy for moving ahead'.[4]

There are other benefits. For instance, writing in 1971, Saul Alinsky complains that 'effective organizing is thwarted by the desire for instant and dramatic change... to go right in to the third act, skipping the first two.'[5] Thinking of campaigns in stages helps guard against this. It also helps to address the opposite problem of campaign groups being too meek to confront at all.

The four stages of 'Consciousness', 'Co-ordination', 'Confrontation' and 'Consolidation' can be seen in action in many campaigns, including in the long struggle for universal suffrage in Britain.

Corresponding and responding

1789 was a year of revolution. In France, Parisians stormed the Bastille – one in a series of events that led to the overthrow of the monarchy and the first elections in Europe in which a majority of men could vote. Over the Atlantic, revolutionary leader George Washington became the first President of the United States. Meanwhile, in Britain, things seemed much as they always had been. The *haves* held the power and the *have nots* were excluded. This was clearly reflected in the method for deciding who could and could not vote for members of Parliament. Only 10 per cent of people could vote, and the ballot was based on privilege. It was far from secret. The number of people represented by one MP differed sharply. Some seats in Parliament could effectively be bought and sold, while others were in the gift of the local aristocrat, and some new industrial cities such as Manchester and Birmingham were not represented at all.

In 1791, Tom Paine catalyzed the Consciousness Stage of the campaign by publishing *The Rights of Man* – a work penned to set the record straight in response to a book by Edmund Burke that had attacked the ideals of the French Revolution. *The Rights of Man* logically and accessibly laid out the argument that all men are born equal and that the constitution should reflect this (women were not mentioned). In the first part he argued for equal political rights and in the second – published in 1792 – for economic rights as well.[6] In so doing, he caught the nation's mood. The establishment felt threatened and Paine was accused of seditious libel – at which point he escaped to France.

Paine's ideas were not new. In many ways, *The Rights of Man* built on the work of John Cartwright, whose book *The Legislative Rights of the Commonality Vindicated* had been published in 1776. Paine's unique contribution was to present the arguments using a writing style which was easy for the majority of people to understand. Another way of expressing this is to say that it was Paine who helped translate the *potential* power of ideas into Idea Counterpower. Within six months, hundreds of thousands of copies of his book had been sold. One of Paine's critics noted with alarm that 'the friends of insurrection, infidelity and vice carried their exertions so far as to load asses with their pernicious pamphlets and to get them dropped not only in cottages and in highways, but into mines and coalpits'.[7]

Following his arrest for selling Paine's book on street corners, fellow radical Thomas Spence established a radical newspaper called *Pigs' Meat* (named in response to a reference by Burke to 'The Swinish Multitude'). In *Pigs' Meat*, Spence incited his readers to revolution. In one passage he proclaimed: 'Awake! Arise! Arm yourselves with truth, justice, reason. Lay siege to corruption. Claim as your inalienable right, universal suffrage and annual parliaments. And whenever you have the gratification to choose a representative, let him be from among the lower orders of men, and he will know how to sympathize with you.'[8] *Pigs' Meat* was just one of many small publications produced by activists.

The first group that emerged to co-ordinate the campaign for parliamentary reform was the Society for Constitutional Information, formed by Cartwright in 1780. This consisted of upper-class intellectuals spreading information about the importance of extending the vote. In 1792, a group broke away, seeking to turn these ideas into action. They called themselves the Society of the Friends of the People and included in their ranks many Whig MPs, including Charles Grey (later not only to become Prime Minister, but to have a kind of tea named after him).

It was also in 1792 that a small group of workers called a public meeting on the subject of parliamentary reform. The historian EP Thompson describes what happened: 'In the first month of its existence the society debated for five nights in succession the question "Have we, who are Tradesmen, Shopkeepers, and Mechanics, any right to obtain a Parliamentary Reform?" turning it over "in every point of view in which we were capable of presenting the subject to our minds". They decided that they had.'[7] They formed what they called the London Corresponding Society. They passed resolutions and collected petitions in favor of universal manhood suffrage and also contacted similar groups in other cities.

In 1792 the young Grey put a motion before parliament calling for reform. It was easily defeated by the governing Tories. In 1793 he tried again. It was defeated again. With their only method for change exhausted, the Friends of the People disbanded.

The other campaigners bravely continued. Despite sedition trials of their leaders, they defied the authorities by clubbing together to put on a mass conference called the 'British Convention' in Edinburgh later that year, in order to co-ordinate their activities better. The event was convened by Scottish campaigners for universal suffrage, including one Thomas Muir. The Convention was seen by the government of the day as a direct challenge to its authority, even a revolutionary government-in-waiting. But the movement was still weak. The government responded to the British Convention by moving in to arrest those whom they considered to be its ringleaders.

In the Treason Trials that ensued, a number of organizers were condemned to 14 years' transportation. Explaining his decision, the judge declared that 'The British constitution is the best that ever was since the creation of the world, and it is not possible to make it better. Yet Mr Muir has gone among the ignorant country people and told them Parliamentary Reform was absolutely necessary for preserving their liberty.'[9]

The outcome of the 1794 Treason Trials resulted in the end of the Society for Constitutional Information. The Corresponding Societies struggled on, using what Idea Counterpower they could muster, despite a string of Acts of Parliament designed to obstruct them. In 1793, Habeas Corpus was suspended, ostensibly because of the war with France, meaning that activists could be detained without trial. Finally, in 1799, the government passed the 'Corresponding Societies Act', explicitly outlawing campaigning for the extension of the vote. The Corresponding Societies were forced to end their activities.

The movement was thus barely able to pass through the Consciousness Stage of the campaign before it was crushed. But the activities during that time created a base of Idea Counterpower for future campaigns to build on. All of the strands of the movement spread their ideas through books, pamphlets, radical newspapers and public meetings. However, the Corresponding Societies went beyond this by educating themselves through dialogue and co-learning. Their methods were not dissimilar to those of the Brazilian educationalist Paulo Freire, who further developed such methods in the 1960s. He argued that although received definitions of intelligence tend to be situated in the language and culture of the powerful, every person has within them great knowledge. By reaching it, he believed people would realize the causes of their own oppression and find ways to address it – he called this the attainment of critical consciousness.

Although in the end there was little opportunity to develop

tactics beyond the realms of Idea Counterpower, the ideas of those seeking the vote – and the ways in which they were promulgated – were very powerful indeed and far less easily imprisoned than the movement's leaders.

Rising like lions

The struggle for the vote gained momentum again in 1815, when the government introduced a bill quite unrelated to the constitution. The bill was designed to protect the incomes of the wealthy landowners who profited from the growing of wheat. There were riots across the country as the bill went through Parliament, as people realized that the effect would be a significant increase in the price of bread. The legislation, officially known as the 'Importation Act', was commonly referred to as 'the Corn Laws'.

A radical named William Cobbett saw the opportunity to raise the consciousness of the masses, by arguing that the cause of their economic woes was misgovernment, and that the solution was parliamentary reform. Cobbett had begun his political life as a Tory, but had been influenced (amongst other things) by the Idea Counterpower of the early campaigners for the vote. Now he was to spread those ideas much further. As material grievances with the government grew, the cycle of mass public meetings recommenced.

In parallel, self-education groups emerged. Like the Corresponding Societies before them, their methods were what might today be termed 'Freirean'. According to a report by an attendee at a meeting of the 'Stockport Union for the Promotion of Human Happiness', participants would spend the first part of the meeting reading from radical publications of the day such as *Black Dwarf* or the *Manchester Observer*. This would be followed by a discussion debating the words they had read. However, they went further – they taught reading, writing and arithmetic too. One agitator had a particularly large following amongst the attendees of the radical Sunday Schools. Some even wore his portrait around their necks concealed in small lockets. That man was Henry ('Orator') Hunt.

The popular press sought to undermine the campaigners by mocking the ragged and dirty appearance of many of the participants. The figurehead of this re-energized movement could, however, be accused of no such thing. Hunt's trademark was a white top hat, which he said represented the purity of his cause. Nevertheless, the government responded with a smear campaign, accusing him of being unpatriotic. It then resorted to physical power when military officers assaulted Hunt on a visit to Manchester in January 1819, alleging that he had hissed during a rendition of the national anthem.

The movement's Idea Counterpower was clearly beginning to cause discomfort in the high offices of state, as parliamentary records of the period reveal. In a report presented to Parliament in July 1819, magistrates declared that 'desperate demagogues' were preparing for an insurrection by 'attributing their calamities not to any event which cannot be controlled, but to the general measures of government and parliament'. However, as they had no proof of any campaigners breaking the law, they declared themselves 'at a loss how to stem the influence of the dangerous and seditious doctrines which are continually disseminated'.[10]

Not long after, they found a way, based on their Physical Power. In anticipation of a large march and rally by pro-suffrage campaigners planned for 16 August 1819 in Manchester, the magistrates applied for armed 'special constables' to police the event. Amongst the volunteers were 11 mill owners, 7 butchers and 13 publicans. In the words of a contemporary commentator they were 'the city's business mafia on horseback'.[11] To make things worse, they were drunk.

For most of the day's protest hardly a horse rider was seen. The first sign of trouble appeared at the rally. As Hunt began to speak, the men on horseback approached. He suggested that the crowd gave the approaching riders three cheers. But the riders were in no mood for such banter, and charged. In his memoirs,

Manchester activist Samuel Bamford describes what happened next: 'For a moment the crowd held back as in a pause, then was a rush heavy and resistless as a headlong sea; and a sound like low thunder, with screams, prayers and imprecations'.[10] Within 10 minutes the space had been cleared except for the piles of the dead and wounded, surrounded by trampled and bloody hats, shoes and flags. Eleven people were killed and 400 were injured. The incident became known as the 'Peterloo Massacre'.

That night the Confrontation Stage began. Battles raged all night in slum areas of the city as stones were thrown and soldiers responded with gunfire. By the following day, there were riots in the neighboring areas of Stockport and Macclesfield, followed by further battles in Manchester a few days later.[11]

Bamford and Hunt were supporters of nonviolent resistance. But that was not true of the whole of the movement. A significant minority called for an armed uprising. Indeed, Bamford's memoir describes working people all around him 'grinding scythes, others old hatchets, others rusty screwdrivers, rusty swords, pikels and mop nails, anything which could be made to cut or stab was pronounced fit for service'.[10] But they were never used. Henry Hunt, trying to operate within the existing constitution, ordered that any planned uprising should not go ahead. The movement turned to bitter infighting and acrimony. This was exacerbated when a government *agent provocateur* persuaded a group to arrange to kill a number of government ministers but then exposed the plot before it could happen.[12] The movement lost its momentum and many of the pro-suffrage groups disbanded.

The confrontation turned to consolidation again, as it was recognized how little could be won while the hostile government of Lord Liverpool remained in power. Although the movement did not win this round of the struggle for the extension of the vote, it did not lose either. The protest was to have an important effect. The illegitimacy of the state had been unveiled and a greater feeling of injustice grew amongst the laboring classes.

Another famous legacy of the Peterloo massacre came in the form of a poem by Percy Shelley, who was deeply moved by reports of the incident. He immediately set to writing an epic poem retelling the events of the day. The final verse has inspired opposition movements ever since:

Rise like lions after slumber
In unvanquishable number
Shake your chains to earth like dew
Which in sleep hath fallen upon you
For we are many, they are few

Once again, the government had succeeded in crushing the movement with its physical power. Once again, the movement had responded by promulgating ideas that continued to grow. However, in the short term the energies of radicals turned from the cause of political reform to the cause of trade union organizing. They might not have known it, but this was to be an important step towards winning universal suffrage.

Representation of the people

A vital part of the Consciousness Stage of the battle for the vote was a burgeoning alternative press. In the early 19th century a number of radical newspapers were produced which served both to give an alternative viewpoint to the established media and to advertise the growing number of radical meetings. Bound copies of *Poor Man's Advocate*, *Gorgon* and *Voice of the People* live on today in archives and libraries,[13] telling the story of the social struggles of the time from an activist's perspective.

In order to stifle the circulation of such subversive commentary, the government introduced a tax to put them outside the purchasing power of ordinary working people and newspapers were supposed to carry a 'stamp' to show that the duty had been paid. One of the newspapers that refused to pay the inhibitive tax was *The Poor Man's Guardian*. Its first issue declared: 'We will try, step by step, the power of RIGHT against MIGHT, and we will begin by protecting and upholding this grand bulwark and defense of all our rights – this key to all our liberties – the freedom of the press.'

The Poor Man's Guardian constructed its own stamp, whose logo incorporated the phrase 'Liberty of the Press' and was emblazoned with some timeless words that encapsulate the notion of Idea Counterpower: 'Knowledge is Power'. Despite 740 people coming to trial for selling such unstamped publications, the newspaper reached 20,000 people every week. After a number of years, their disobedience led to change as the tax was reduced from four pence to one penny.

The unstamped press clearly represents the use of Idea Counterpower at the Consciousness Stage. But the meetings that they advertised within signaled the Co-ordination Stage, as they told people about the meetings for the vote and of trade unions. When the growing workers' movement maintained its commitment to parliamentary reform, the cause had the option of Economic Counterpower in its toolbox.

However, it was Physical Counterpower that characterized the greatest clashes of the Confrontation Stage – not in the cities, but in the countryside. The industrial revolution had hurt rural workers badly. Wages had plummeted and conditions worsened. In the early 1830s, parish rates were used in many places in Britain to top up starvation wages. This was effectively a subsidy to the employer – and even the benefit of this declined, as it was spread more and more thinly.

With those using only Idea Counterpower being ignored or crushed, and insufficient co-ordination to utilize Economic Counterpower, agricultural workers used the only option they had left – physical resistance. In many counties, including Kent, Surrey, Sussex and Wiltshire, farm laborers rose up to surround the houses of the exploitative landowners, to burn hayricks and to dismantle threshing machinery in protest at their declining wages. The wave of unrest spread to surrounding counties. The government arrested some 1,900 agricultural campaigners, eventually hanging 19 of them, transporting 481, and imprisoning 644.[14] Letters outlining agriculturalists' demands were signed 'Captain Swing', leading to the actions being dubbed the 'Swing Riots'. However, even the most conservative politicians must have been able to see that something had to be done to neutralize this force.

In an unrelated turn of events, a parliamentary fall-out over the emancipation of Catholics led to the Duke of Wellington being ejected from office, to be replaced by the very same Charles (now Earl) Grey who had proposed the first suffrage bill some 40 years before. Finally, the movement had a usable balance of insider and outsider power. There was a reformer in government, able to lever change at the heart of the system, and a strong outsider movement to ensure that he did so. Grey drew up a Reform Bill promising to extend the vote to males owning or renting property worth £10 and to redistribute seats in line with population, so that each vote would be more proportionately equal.

But the Bill still left the vast majority of the population disenfranchised. Although some saw this as a positive move, not everyone fell for the trap of getting behind the government. On 3 December 1831, The *Poor Man's Guardian* editorialized: 'It is now pretty well understood, we trust, that the measure gives nothing to you: but it is considered that it will be a "stepping stone", to something that will do you good. Now the only ground upon which it can possibly be so considered is that the reformed constitution will be more favorable to your interests than the present, or rather that the £10 householders or "middlemen" who are to acquire a voice in the government, will be more inclined to admit your right to universal suffrage.'[15]

On the other hand, many parliamentarians did not want to give up even the limited power they would cede through the Reform Act, despite a wish to put down the growing protest movement in the country. The bill received a majority of only one on its second reading and was amended at the committee stage. Grey saw this as a defeat and opted to dissolve parliament and stand for re-election. He was re-elected with an increased majority, despite the corrupt system. When the House of Lords rejected his bill again, however, the outsider movements took to the streets and refused to be ignored. In Bristol the demonstrations turned to riots that lasted for three days. Four demonstrators were subsequently executed.[9]

Grey made further compromises for the House of Lords, but the second chamber nevertheless blocked it once again. As before, Grey resigned. When he did, mass meetings erupted in every town. Movement leaders espoused proposals for mass civil disobedience, including removal of money from the banks in protest. The King [William IV] requested that Grey return in order to quell the chaos. Grey pledged only to do so if the King created enough new Lords to allow the bill through the second chamber. Eventually he didn't have to. The threat that the existing Lords' power might be diluted was sufficient that they let the bill through. The co-ordinated movement and the confrontation were therefore enough to get the Representation of the People Act (better known as the first Reform Act) passed.

Nevertheless, this was very much a compromise. While the movement was demanding 100-per-cent male suffrage, the Reform Bill of 1832 extended it to just 18 per cent of adult men. The changes extended power to a small extent, but it did not redistribute it, nor did it rid the voting system of corruption.

The new arrangement brought some changes long called for by Counterpower movements. For example, in 1833 the Slavery Abolition Act was passed, then strengthened in 1838, after a campaign that had lasted 40 years. In 1847, a bill limiting the work of women and children in factories to 10 hours a day was passed following intense agitation by socialists and trade-unionists. Both of these parliamentary victories would have been impossible under the previous regime.

Despite these steps forward, the Reform Bill was only a fraction of what the movement had demanded, and became known as the 'Great Betrayal'. A group including *Poor Man's Guardian* editor Henry Hetherington began setting the stage for another organization to emerge.

The Chartists

In 1838, new groups called 'Working Men's Associations' drew up what they called the 'People's Charter', a simple manifesto for the next period of struggle that would, in their own words, 'Place all classes of society in possession of their equal, political and social rights'. They became known as Chartists.

Once again, the Consciousness and Co-ordination Stages restarted, as campaigners toured the country with a simple manifesto. Its demands were as follows:

1) A vote for all men over the age of 21
2) A secret ballot
3) Electoral districts of equal size
4) No property qualification to become an MP
5) Payment for MPs
6) Annual elections for parliament.[9]

While these aims were never to be realized in the life-spans of the Working Men's Associations, today we see five of the six accepted as common sense.

In the first year of the movement, the Chartists gathered well over a million signatures for their People's Charter, but nevertheless Parliament rejected it. This led to a major split in the movement, between those who advocated the continuation of 'moral 'suasion' (Idea Counterpower), led by William Lovett, and those led by Feargus O'Connor who argued for 'physical force' (Physical Counterpower) in the form of an armed uprising.

The section of the movement most sympathetic to more violent action was concentrated in South Wales. In 1839, a band of agitators toured the area, mobilizing discontented people, and gathered forces to march on Newport. There they planned to rescue Henry Vincent (a prominent Chartist who had been jailed) and seize the town. Reports of the action portray a chaotic affair as all element of surprise was lost by their loud approach. Arriving in the city, they approached the Westgate Hotel, where soldiers were staying. The marchers demanded that the soldiers 'Surrender Our Prisoners' – a request which was refused. As a police officer attempted to seize a rifle, it was accidentally fired. The shot was the signal for a general charge upon the building and the police line (armed only with staves) broke. Activists smashed windows and climbed through. Soldiers fired on the protesters. Shrieks of the dying and wounded filled the air and the crowd dispersed. Twenty Chartists were killed that day. Soon afterwards, the South Wales Chartist leaders were captured and sentenced.[14]

Meanwhile, the advocates of 'moral 'suasion' continued their petitioning. They garnered ever more support as Chartist demands were mixed with the concerns of the nascent trade unions and the Irish Home Rule movement. A new petition presented in 1842 had more than three million signatures but it was rejected by Parliament once again. In response, more than half a million people from different industries marched out on strike. This was aided as people in some areas toured factories literally 'pulling the plug' on the steam engines so that they could not work. The 'Plug Plot' was Britain's first general strike. It was overwhelmed by state physical power as thousands were arrested. The Confrontation Stage once again turned to Consolidation. The movement died down. The Working Men's Associations eventually closed their doors in 1860. They thought they had lost. But in fact they were closer to success than anyone could have imagined.

The Reform League

One of the people influenced by the activities of the Chartists and the oratory of Henry Hunt before them was the MP John Bright. Bright had already made a name for himself for his role in campaigning against the Corn Laws. In 1865, he helped set up the Reform League, which started the cycle of Consciousness and Co-ordination once again.

When the police attempted to close down public gatherings of the Reform League in Hyde Park, this turned to Confrontation. But the demonstrators were not in the mood to be stopped. Unfazed by police lines, protesters pulled down the fence in order to assemble where they had planned to.

This was the perfect opportunity for reformers in parliament to force the resignation of Home Secretary Spencer Walpole. With the momentum built, they followed this up with a second Reform Act in 1867. This Act extended the vote to another two million people, including male heads of urban households and some lodgers. It also enfranchised a number of towns which had grown during the Industrial Revolution and had previously had no parliamentary representation.

The supporters of the status quo were on the back foot. Walter Bagehot, for example, wrote of his worries about extending the vote to the 'ignorant masses': 'What I fear is that both our political parties will bid for the support of the working man: and that both will promise to do as he likes'.[16] As the population became more and more empowered, that is what began to happen, as the hand of the reformers in Parliament was strengthened. In comparatively quick succession, Parliament passed legislation on many of the major calls of the movement, including the introduction of the secret ballot in parliamentary elections (1872) and giving the vote to male heads of households in the countryside (1884). Power was being redistributed. Yet it took almost 100 years from the founding of the Corresponding Societies to reach even the partial democratization of the late 19th century, by which time 60 per cent of men could vote. And another long campaign was yet to be won. That was the campaign for female suffrage.

Votes for Women

Throughout the time of the movement for the vote for working men, the Consciousness Stage of another campaign was brewing: the campaign for the extension of the vote to women. It can be traced right back to the year following the publication of *The Rights of Man*, when an even more radical pamphlet was released: *A Vindication of the Rights of Woman*, by Mary Wollstonecraft, which argued that men and women were equal in the eyes of God, and therefore should have equal rights. In the run-up to the Peterloo Massacre, women's-suffrage societies were formed. Women also voted in the meetings of both sexes. Indeed, it was Samuel Bamford, whose memoirs were quoted earlier, who proposed this idea. When he put forward the resolution that women should be allowed to vote at their meetings, the women did not wait to be given permission. They raised their arms in agreement with the motion, and from then on always voted at the radical meetings.[10] During the Chartist campaign, too, a significant minority argued that both women and men should be allowed to vote.

Women did persuade some men to place petitions and motions before the House of Commons. In 1832, Henry Hunt asked the House of Commons to consider the idea, which even he prefaced by warning it 'may be a subject of mirth to some Hon Gentlemen'.[17]

In 1867 Harriet Taylor persuaded John Stuart Mill to propose an amendment to the 1867 Reform Bill, proposing to replace the word 'man' with 'person' throughout the document. But without a sufficient Counterpower movement, parliament rejected both these ideas by a large margin. In this context, early feminists worked to address other aspects of imbalances of power between the genders. For example, the period saw successful campaigns for women to be able to enter universities and the professions. In 1867 the National Society for Women's Suffrage was formed, which won an early publicity coup when a clerical error meant that a widowed shopkeeper from Manchester named Lily Maxwell found herself on the electoral register. Unfortunately, a short while later the courts declared voting by women illegal.

The lawyer representing Lily Maxwell was Richard Pankhurst, a Liberal who later joined the Independent Labour

Party (ILP). Throughout the latter part of the 19th century, Pankhurst and various radical MPs continued their attempts to amend and propose legislation in Parliament. They did win some minor victories – for example, women ratepayers won the right to vote in local elections in 1869. But on the whole, those with power attempted to block them at every turn.

This even applied to the holding of public assemblies. In 1896 a bitter dispute took place between Manchester City Council and the ILP about whether they could hold public meetings at Boggart Hole Clough – a green space in the city. When two ILP members refused to pay the fines imposed upon them for 'occasioning an annoyance', they were sent to prison. The ILP defied the authorities by calling another assembly in the park with 40,000 attendees. The speakers included party leader Keir Hardie, Richard Pankhurst, his young wife Emmeline and two of their teenage daughters – Christabel and Sylvia.[18]

In 1897, Millicent Fawcett co-ordinated the formation of the National Union of Women's Suffrage Societies. This was the group that became more popularly known as the 'Suffragists' – committed only to those ways of campaigning that fell within the law. The Suffragists wrote letters to politicians, requested meetings, collected petitions and organized public meetings. Yet such Idea Counterpower alone could not build a critical mass for change. Richard Pankhurst died in 1898. But, inspired by the defiance of the Boggart Hole Clough campaign, his wife and daughters fought on. Unimpressed by the reformism of the NUWSS, they invited a number of female members of the ILP to their house. There they decided to pursue a more militant approach. They formed the Women's Social and Political Union. According to one campaigner, it was because of this organization that the 'smoldering resentment in women's hearts burst into the flame of revolt'.[19]

The beginning of the Confrontation Stage can be traced to a public meeting addressed by the MP Sir Edward Grey at Manchester's Free Trade Hall in 1905. Hearing that a group of Liberals was to gather there, the young law student Christabel

Pankhurst and her companion Annie Kenney decided to make their voices heard.[20]

Christabel Pankhurst recounts what happened next in her autobiography: 'Calm but with beating hearts we took our seats and looked at the exultant throng we must soon anger by our challenge. Their cheers as the speakers entered gave us the note and pitch of their emotion... Annie as the Working Woman – for this should make the stronger appeal to the Liberals – rose first and asked "Will the Liberal Government give Votes for Women?" No answer came. I joined my voice to hers and our banner was unfurled, making clear what was our question. The effect was explosive. The meeting was aflame with excitement.'[21]

As the women were removed by the police, Christabel turned and spat at the officer apprehending her. It is likely that this was no rash act, but a carefully thought-out act of defiance, calculated to reach the morning papers. It did. The militant women had begun to show women standing up for themselves, and in so doing helped to raise the consciousness of a generation. The *Daily Mail* decided to mockingly term the new militant group the 'Suffragettes'. The name stuck.

Annie Kenney's memoir picks up the story: 'Christabel Pankhurst had declared war. Her army consisted of her mother, her two sisters, Miss Billington, myself and about 20 working women who had broken away from the Labour Party to devote themselves to the cause. Her opponents' army consisted of two highly organized political parties, Liberal and Conservative, of the Labour Party, whose support was here today, gone tomorrow, of the whole press, and of practically all women's societies.'[22]

The next confrontational tactic was a militant election policy: campaigning against all government ministers unless they promised to support votes for women. This manifested itself in a campaign to persuade the young cabinet minister Winston Churchill to introduce Votes for Women into the Conservative program. When quizzed on the subject at a public meeting, he replied: 'Nothing would induce me to vote for giving women the franchise and I am not going to be henpecked into a question of such grave importance'.[22]

As women were not able to speak in government or parliament through constitutional means, they found other ways to make their way into the corridors of power. This included a number of 'rushes' – whereby women would attempt to enter physically by any means possible. When the Prime Minister refused an invitation to meet the campaigners, Annie Kenney headed a delegation to Downing Street. One woman rang on the bell, while another engaged the police in conversation. As soon as the door was open, the women attempted to barge through. In another instance, two women chained themselves to the grille of Westminster's Ladies Gallery and addressed Parliament from there.

As the movement broadened, it also split. Frustrated by the over-central role of the Pankhursts, another equally militant group was formed, who named themselves the Women's Freedom League, while the constitutionalist sister organization the NUWSS also continued its activities. Annie Kenney's memoir acknowledges the differences of opinion between the organizations, but writes that the different strands were 'as one from a strategic point of view'. Indeed, the Suffragists and Suffragettes did on occasion work together to organize mass demonstrations. Many constitutionalists also offered shelter, food and comfort for the militants on their way in and out of prison. They were able to maintain their Co-ordination in order for the Confrontation to be effective.

Growing militancy

As this new wave of angry, eloquent and skilful women stood at polling booths and sold their newspaper *Votes for Women*, they were often met with opprobrium. Rotten eggs and rubbish were thrown at them and men would on occasion pretend to mistake them for prostitutes. In some towns Suffragettes were taken to the police station for their own security. At a public meeting in Sutton, rats were released in order to remove a female campaigner. But still they continued.

As the Suffragettes gained ground, supporters of the status quo were forced to defend their stance. Lord Cromer, leader of the National League for Opposing Women's Suffrage gave the following four reasons:

> *Because I consider the measure fraught with danger to the British Empire*
> *Because it would be subversive to peace in our homes*
> *Because it flies in face of nature, which has clearly indicated the spheres of action respectively assigned to the two sexes*
> *Because those who make the laws should have the physical force to enforce them, and this women do not possess.*[23]

After five years of confrontation, women were unofficially promised the vote, pending a truce in militant action, ahead of the General Election of 1910. Yet no such bill was included in the legislative program. Some sympathetic male MPs were finally persuaded to draw up 'The Conciliation Bill'. When this fell too, the women's anger turned to still greater militancy, this time even more determinedly designed to undermine the power of those who ruled.

One track of action was tax resistance – some women refused to pay tax if they were to be given no representation. Then, in 1912, Suffragettes began breaking windows[24] – Emmeline Pankhurst pronounced that 'the argument of the broken pane of glass is the most valuable argument in modern politics'.[25] Another tack was to damage the property of the rich, including empty mansions, theaters and cricket pavilions. The new phase even included the posting of inflammable chemicals to Chancellor of the Exchequer Lloyd George and an attack on his partially constructed house. In her new publication *The Suffragette*,[26] Christabel editorialized: 'Women will never get the vote except by creating an intolerable situation for all the selfish and apathetic people who stand in their way'.[27]

The tactics of the militants were an intense source of frustration for constitutionalists. Millicent Fawcett called them 'the meat and drink of the anti-suffragists'.[28] Philip Snowden – a member of the Men's Union for Women's Suffrage (and later Chancellor of the Exchequer in Ramsay MacDonald's government) – goes further, writing in his memoirs that 'When they began to destroy property and risk the lives of others than themselves, the public began to turn against them. The National Union of Woman's Suffrage Societies, whose gallant educational and constitutional work for women's freedom had been carried on for more than 50 years, publicly dissociated themselves from these terrorist activities.'[29]

The state's campaign against them intensified. Christabel succeeded in escaping to Paris, leaving Annie Kenney to run the headquarters in London. Other Suffragettes were rounded up and put in prison. There they went on hunger strike, were force-fed and then, when this did not work, were released (amidst much publicity) to eat, before being put in prison again. In a letter to *The Suffragette*, Keir Hardie wrote: 'Women, worn and weak by hunger, are seized upon, held down by brute force, gagged, a tube inserted down their throats and food poured or pumped into the stomach.'[30] It is likely that he heard these stories at first hand. Hardie's life-long friendship with Sylvia Pankhurst had blossomed into romance.

Opportunities to introduce votes for women came and went in the House of Commons. The militancy of the Suffragettes was cited by some MPs as their reason for not supporting the cause. It is impossible to know whether they would have supported the cause had the movement adopted different tactics. What is clear is that the campaign as a whole made a difference – as Parliament had gone from seeing votes for women as a 'subject of some mirth' to a hotly debated topic. A letter from a Suffragette published in the *Daily Telegraph* in 1913 summed up the choice that the government faced:

'1: Kill every woman in the United Kingdom

2: Give women the vote.'[31]

But just as the Confrontation Stage was reaching its peak, it was suddenly brought to an end. On the outbreak of the First World War the WSPU suspended its militancy. For its part the state released the Suffragette women from their prison cells. But the campaigners for women's suffrage had already changed the balance of power in society. They would finally taste the fruits of their labor in the Consolidation Stage.

Women and war

The commencement of the First World War in 1914 brought a new rapprochement between Suffragettes and the government. Emmeline and Christabel turned their attentions to speaking tours urging young men to sign up and fight. Their condemnation of socialist and pacifist opponents of war and their repeated appeals against strikes won them some unusual admirers. Amongst them was Lord Northcliffe – conservative proprietor of *The Times* and the *Daily Mail*. The new approach also brought Emmeline and Christabel into alliance with another recent foe – David Lloyd George.

A significant problem for Lloyd George, who became Prime Minister in 1916, was the shortage of labor in the munitions factories caused by the number of young men leaving their jobs in order to sign up as soldiers. An obvious solution to this was the employment of women. But in order to win social permission for such a change, and to offset the potential of opposition from trades unions, he needed to show demand. The Suffragettes gave him a way to do that. At the instigation (and with the funding) of the government, Emmeline helped to organize a march in London calling for women's employment in the munitions factories.[27]

This was not the approach of all Suffragettes. For example, the younger Pankhurst sisters Sylvia and Adela perceived the actions of Christabel and Emmeline as jingoistic and wrong. Resident in Australia at the time, Adela was part of the successful campaign against conscription in that country before taking a job as an organizer of the Victoria Socialist Party.

Sylvia had already broken with the WSPU in 1913, unhappy with the arson campaign. She turned to working more closely with working-class communities in London's East End, where she helped to establish a number of practical projects alleviating the suffering of some of the city's worst-off people. Her projects included women-and-baby clinics, a Montessori school and a cost-price restaurant. Her newspaper *Women's Dreadnought* tracked the declining living conditions as prices and rents rose. Over the course of the war, she increasingly saw the cause of women's oppression in class terms instead of merely as a question of gender. This was reflected in a change in the title of her organization to the Workers' Suffrage Federation, then the Workers' Socialist Federation – campaigning for the extension of the vote and the redistribution of economic power to working-class people – be they women or men. Her newspaper changed its name too – to *Workers' Dreadnought*. Accused of sedition, her writings later led to her being jailed again.

Given greater impetus by events in Russia, the broader socialist movement with which Sylvia associated steadily grew. The inequalities in British society were more clearly reflected than ever, as hundreds of thousands of working-class men were sent to die for their government without even having had a say in voting for it. Even before the war, 'The Great Unrest' had been one of the most intense periods of industrial militancy that Britain had ever known. Over the course of the First World War strikes grew from 532 in 1916, to 730 in 1917 and to 1,168 by 1918.[27] Tanks were even dispatched to the streets of Glasgow to put down the protests on 'Red Clydeside'. John MacLean, one of the Scottish Socialist leaders, was a contributor to Sylvia's newspaper. In Leeds a workers' soviet was established, which called on the country to form councils of workers and soldiers in the image of those in Russia and Germany. Even as the Women's Suffrage movement was at its Consolidation Stage, the radical workers' movement was becoming ever more confrontational. The timing was fortuitous.

The government began preparing an Act to introduce near-universal male suffrage, including setting the voting age for men at 21. Millicent Fawcett formed a delegation to request that women should also be enfranchised in this bill. Despite protests from some constitutionalists, the delegation included Emmeline Pankhurst. The group was willing to compromise in its demands and, in order to pacify the Conservatives upon whose votes the Act would rely, it accepted a host of conditions. The tactic paid off. On the day, 387 MPs voted for the Women's Clause, with only 87 opposing it.[27] As a result, in addition to bringing about the vote for men, the Representation of the People Act 1918 extended the right to vote to women over 30 who were householders, the wives of householders, occupiers of property with an annual rent of £5 or graduates of British universities. All women in the UK were finally granted the right to vote on the same basis as men in 1928.

For Fawcett's Suffragists, the 1918 victory was testament to decades of constitutional campaigns for change. For Emmeline and Christabel, it reflected the delayed gains from their militant strategy. For Sylvia and other radicals, the eventual extension of the ballot was a concession by those in power in order to prevent more fundamental change. To an extent they were all right. The Suffragists embodied the Co-ordination Stage, the Suffragettes moved things to the Confrontation Stage, while the Socialists aided the Consolidation Stage. In the process, the perfect dynamics were constructed to achieve a major step towards the change for which they had so long strived.

Thanks to these campaigns, which eventually led to the extension of the vote to almost all working-class adults, feats were possible in the 20th century that would have been unlikely before. In 1945 a cabinet featuring many prominent trade unionists oversaw the introduction of a universal health system, a universal education system, a house-building program and the nationalization of the commanding heights of the economy. Following the Economic Counterpower and Idea Counterpower generated by a strike by women sewing machinists at a Ford plant in 1968, the employment minister Barbara Castle introduced legislation promoting equal pay for equal work in 1970.

Yet despite these important reforms, the battle for gender equality has still not been won. According to the Fawcett Society (successor organization to the NUWSS) women earn on average 15 per cent less than men in Britain.[32] Even by 2011 only 30 per cent of MPs in the British parliament were female. Across the world, women only constitute 20 per cent of parliamentarians. Meanwhile, studies show a link between the arrangement of global trade along neoliberal lines and the further impoverishment of women.[33]

Neither has the redistribution of political opportunity for men and women fully translated into the redistribution of economic opportunity, as rich élites have found other ways of maintaining their power – including through ownership of the media, promulgation of rightwing ideologies and the co-opting of the institutions of the center left. As early as in 1918, Sylvia Pankhurst declared that, were a Labour government to be elected, it 'would be swept along in the wake of a capitalist policy'.[27] Her prediction proved prescient long into the future. Following the rise of neo-liberalism in the 1980s and 1990s, every mainstream political party in Britain signed up to capitalism's most extreme manifestation. This wasn't a phenomenon exclusive to Britain, but was reflected in many countries of the world. But almost as soon as the new ideology took hold, new forms of resistance began emerging, as the following chapter will show.

1 Chris Rose, *How to Win Campaigns*, Earthscan, London, 2005. **2** Including 'The Four Stages of the Revolutionary Process' by RD Hopper, 'The Movement Action Plan' by Bill Moyer, 'The Issue Attention Cycle' conceived of by Anthony Downs and the four stages of social movements summarized by John Maclonis. **3** Joe Slovo et al, *Southern Africa: The New Politics of Revolution*, Penguin, London, 1976. **4** Bill Moyer, *The Movement Action Plan*, 1987. **5** Saul Alinsky, *Rules for Radicals: A Pragmatic Primer for Realistic Radicals*, Vintage, Toronto, 1971. **6** Thomas Paine, *The*

Rights of Man. **7** EP Thompson, *The Making of the English Working Class,* Penguin, London, 1980. **8** Spartacus, *Excerpt from Pigs Meat,* available at nin.tl/r6KVBt **9** Mike Ashley, *Taking Liberties: The Struggle for Britain's Freedoms and Rights,* British Library, London, 2008. **10** Samuel Bamford, *Passages in the Life of a Radical,* Oxford Paperbacks, Oxford, 1984. **11** Paul Mason, *Live Working or Die Fighting: How the Working Class Went Global,* Random House, London, 2006. **12** Known as the Cato Street Conspiracy. **13** For example, the Working Class Movement Library in Salford. **14** Rob Sewell, *In the Cause of Labour: History of British Trade Unionism,* Wellred, London, 2003. **15** *The Poor Man's Guardian,* 3 Dec 1831 in *The Poor Man's Guardian 1831-1835,* Merlin Press, 1969. **16** Quoted in Sewell, op cit. **17** Hansard Parliamentary Debates, 3rd Series: Vol XIV, 3 Aug 1832. **18** Joyce Marlow (ed), *Votes for Women: The Virago Book of Suffragettes,* Virago, London, 2000.
19 Hannah Mitchell, quoted in Marlow, op cit. **20** There is some speculation that the relationship between Christabel and Annie – who lived together – was more than just political. However nothing in either autobiography confirms this to be the case. **21** Christabel Pankhurst, *Unshackled,* reprinted in Marlow, op cit. **22** Annie Kenney, *Memoirs of a Militant,* Edward Arnold, London, 1924. **23** Lord Cromer, *The Danger of Woman Suffrage,* in Marlow, op cit. **24** For a first-hand account see Charlotte Marsh, 'Militant Memories', in Marlow, op cit. **25** Quoted in Marlow, op cit. **26** Following a split with some other Suffragettes who maintained control of *Votes for Women.* **27** Martin Pugh, *The Pankhursts,* Penguin, London, 2001. **28** Millicent Fawcett, *Broken Windows and After,* in Marlow, op cit. **29** Philip Snowden, *An Autobiography,* 1934 excerpt at nin.tl/nQmsZB **30** Keir Hardie, letter to *Votes for Women,* 1 Oct 1909. **31** Bertha Brewster, 'Letter to *The Telegraph*', in Marlow, op cit. **32** The Fawcett Society, *Equal Pay: The Facts,* nin.tl/jvp0LQ **33** One World Action, *Making Trade Work for Women,* www.oneworldaction.org

7
How movements resist corporate power

'*Another world is not only possible, she is on her way. On a quiet day, I can hear her breathing.*'

Arundhati Roy

After centuries of struggle for the redistribution of power within the state, campaigners at the turn of the millennium faced a new challenge. As Joel Bakan's documentary film *The Corporation* puts it: '150 years ago the business corporation was a relatively insignificant institution. Today it is all-pervasive. Like the church, the monarchy and the Communist Party in other times and places, the corporation is today's dominant institution.'

By 1999 a majority of the 100 largest economies in the world were corporations rather than countries and 82 of the biggest 200 firms were from the US. Substantial amounts were spent on direct donations to political parties and yet more to pro-corporate lobbying groups. It would seem that the investment paid off: in the years between 1983 and 1999, profits at the biggest 200 corporations increased by 362.4 per cent.[1]

According to critics, these profits came at a cost to the poor. In the 1980s and 1990s, many countries of the world were witness to mass privatization, reductions in funding for public services, the restriction of trade unions and the watering down of regulations protecting consumers and the environment. The impacts were to be felt on a global scale as the International Monetary Fund and World Bank – in which the US has a controlling stake – spread the approach to the Majority World.

In 1995 another organization was added to the list – the World Trade Organization (WTO), perceived by activists as further committed to stripping away those minimal protections that the people and environment still retained.

But on 30 November 1999 a protest in Seattle began to make the world think differently and gave strength and inspiration to a new generation of activists. 'N30' was not a normal march and rally. It was a determined attempt to close down a meeting of the WTO. The objective of closing down the talks was publicized widely in advance. The authorities didn't believe that the activists would succeed in their aim. Neither did many of the protesters themselves. But they did.

The events helped launch onto the consciousness of the world the existence of what is referred to by many of its participants as the global justice movement. The phrase 'One No, Many Yeses' has often been used to encapsulate the movement's diversity.[2] The 'No' can be described as the economics of neoliberalism along with the deleterious policies flowing out of it. The various 'yeses' include anarchism, democratic regulation, localization, socialism and eco-socialism to name only a few.[3] To my eye though, one idea unites all these 'yeses'. That idea is the redistribution of power from corporations to people. The struggle for the redistribution of power is an idea that connects the global justice movement with many of the movements that precede it. This prompts the question as to whether the lessons of campaigns past can help explain the global justice movement's successes and setbacks.

Answering that question requires a look into the movement's history. Contrary to some accounts, it did not begin in Seattle. The events there could best be viewed as the beginning of the global Confrontation Stage of a movement of movements (each following their own four stages of Counterpower) that had been steadily growing for decades.

The birth of the global justice movement

In common with other examples in this book, corporations gained their dominance through a mixture of idea power, economic power and physical power. Chief amongst these is the promulgation of the ideology of neoliberalism. Research by seminal author-activist Susan George reveals how corporate foundations 'create[d] "debates" out of thin air', and shaped perceptions of what is and is not worthy of research through the establishment of and support for a swathe of pro-corporate thinktanks, academic chairs and journals.[4] By the 1980s many people believed that there was no realistic alternative to neoliberalism.

The rise of the new ideology was amply aided by physical power as the theories were initially put into practice by the US-backed, human-rights-abusing dictator of Chile – General Pinochet. Thereafter they were exported to other authoritarian regimes in Latin America before spreading further afield. Pinochet and others were opposed by social movements calling for human rights, democracy and the redistribution of wealth. But the movements were brutally suppressed and thousands were tortured or killed by the state.[5]

During the 1980s and 1990s, the World Bank and IMF used their economic power to insist on poor countries following 'Structural Adjustment Programs' (SAPs), based on the cornerstones of neoliberalism: privatization, austerity, weak regulation and low tariffs. These gave transnational corporations access to new markets. But that access came at a cost, to the extent that some African social movements suggested that SAP more accurately stood for 'Suffering for African People'. Across the world, those poor countries that most closely embraced global 'free' trade between the late 1980s and late 1990s saw a 24-per-cent increase in the number of people below the poverty line.[6] Meanwhile, many of the countries that succeeded in reducing poverty and inequality did so precisely because they rejected neoliberal policy prescriptions.[7]

Protests against SAPs led to the overthrow of some of the governments which were implementing them. But elections did not bring democracy. The newly elected parliaments were still shackled by the economic power of global capital and the international financial institutions.

In 1990 the African Council of Churches demanded the full cancellation of the poorest countries' debt.[8] Much of the debt had been racked up by illegitimate rulers, many of whom had been installed and supported by the US or USSR during the Cold War. These debts had increased due to a series of external shocks, including the oil crisis. Now oppressed peoples were being impoverished yet more as they were required to 'pay back' the debts at the expense of funds for health and education. A group in Britain responded to the call by forming the Debt Crisis Network, which organized speaker tours to raise awareness of the issue.[9]

In Mexico – a country that had already seen great transfers of wealth and power into the hands of transnational corporations – one group decided to take a rather more militant approach. On the day that the North American Free Trade Agreement came into force, the Zapatista Army for National Liberation instigated an uprising. It was suppressed, but it caught the attention of the world. After petitioning and uprising failed to lead to the adoption of their proposals, the Zapatistas established self-governing autonomous communities in their Chiapas region. Poems and statements by the movement's mythical leader Subcomandante Marcos were read by people across the globe. Here was a movement, on the doorstep of the world's only superpower, showing that another way really was possible.

Meanwhile, in Britain, a group growing out of the roads protests called Reclaim the Streets began imagining how roads without cars and capitalism might look. In 1995, a group of people with sound systems set up an instant street party on London's Camden High Street as a self-managed temporary alternative. More street parties followed, including an occasion when 10,000 people closed down a motorway. Underneath the skirts of stilt-walkers, people drilled holes into the road in order to plant trees, the sound disguised by the music emanating from amplifiers all around them. The leaflets that were distributed proclaimed 'beneath the tarmac, the forest!'

International co-ordination of the diverse struggles against corporate power could be seen as early as 1993, when Latin American farmers joined with their counterparts in Europe to form La Via Campesina – the International Peasant Movement. Then, in 1996, a global meeting called by the Zapatistas led to the creation of People's Global Action two years later: a network with a stated commitment to challenging the institutions of capitalism, imperialism, feudalism, patriarchy, racism and globalization. At its founding conference in Geneva were representatives of the Indian Karnataka State Farmers' Association (involved in direct-action campaigns against Monsanto), MST (the Brazilian landless peasants' movement involved in redistributing land by occupying it), and indigenous movements from Latin America as well as activists from the Global North.

The first proof of the effect of this co-ordination came on 16 May 1998. As leaders of some of the world's richest countries sat down at the table of Group of Eight (G8), and shortly before the WTO was to meet in Geneva, a 'global street party' took place in 24 countries. In Hyderabad, 200,000 agriculturalists took to the streets against the WTO. Another 50,000 people demonstrated in Brasilia.[10] In parallel to the more militant and system-critical anti-globalization movement, 70,000 peaceful debt campaigners formed a human chain around the building where the G8 was to meet. This protest was organized by Jubilee 2000 – a new alliance formed out of the Debt Crisis Network. The G8 was moved to another location at the last minute, leaving the journalists to cover the protests instead.

To coincide with the G8 Summit in Cologne the following year, people in 43 countries took part in a global day of action on 18 June (J18). Stock exchanges were blockaded in Australia and Canada. City centers and financial districts were occupied in the Czech Republic, Israel, Scotland, Italy, the Netherlands, Pakistan, Spain and the US. After occupying the financial center in Montevideo, Uruguayans established a spoof 'trade fair' where people could find out about a number of themes, including child labor, the eroding of local culture, and the effects of consumption. In Nigeria, 10,000 people, many of them from the Niger Delta region, spilled into the streets of the petroleum capital Port Harcourt, in a 'carnival of the oppressed'. Shell offices were blockaded, and signs were changed on a road named after the military leader Sani Abacha – so that for a time it was renamed after Ken Saro-Wiwa, the Ogoni poet and protest leader Abacha had hanged. In Britain, 10,000 people joined a 'Carnival against Capital', which included direct actions against a number of corporations and ended with a huge street party outside the London International Financial Futures Exchange. In a *pièce de resistance* the lower entrance was bricked up while some protesters made their way inside to dismantle equipment.

With the previous actions having proved that the movement was both global and capable of confrontation, it was N30 – the 1999 protests at the WTO in Seattle – that showed this to the world's media. An activist described how people used 'chicken wire, duct tape, PVC piping, chains and padlocks to secure themselves together by joining arms from shoulder to hands. They sat down and took over the intersection, surrounded by their support team. Traffic was effectively blocked in four directions.' The same action was repeated in strategic locations across the city. Meanwhile, a labor march was diverted and a festival of resistance took place in the streets.

The authorities did everything in their power to clear the area: 'Police lifted the protective bandanas worn by locked-down protesters who were sitting in the street and squirted pepper spray directly into their eyes. Other protesters already immobilized by teargas hunched over and huddled together for protection. Their heads were pulled back by their hair and their eyes were purposefully sprayed. They could neither get away nor protect their faces with their hands. Rubber bullets bruised the backs of retreating demonstrators; cans of teargas were thrown indiscriminately into crowds of students who had no place to go.'[11]

Thousands of arrests of nonviolent protesters were made, prompting a vigil at the jail, negotiations with city authorities, solidarity from trade unionists and, eventually, release of the protesters. But the rebellion was not confined to the streets outside. Inside the conference walls, representatives of more than 40 poor nations joined together to speak out against being bullied by rich countries who were disregarding the negative impact on employment, poverty and human rights of the ruthless push for economic liberalization. They were soon backed up by major NGOs, which put out statements condemning the richest countries' practice and the process of the talks.

The events in Seattle live on in the collective memory of activists and have even been turned into a film.[12] But the action wasn't confined to one city alone. There were street protests in Bangalore, Berlin, Brisbane, Cardiff, Limerick, London, Manila, Rome, Prague and Tel Aviv. A statue to the WTO was burned by 500 slum-dwellers in Delhi, dockworkers in California went on strike and in Dijon, France, protesters chained themselves to the railings of the chamber of commerce.[13]

From that point on, every time unaccountable groups of governments met – often in the presence of corporations – the movement was there to make life difficult for them. In 2000, protesters disrupted the World Economic Forum in the Swiss

Alps and again in Melbourne in 2001 – using blockades and street demonstrations which in the latter case succeeded in preventing about a quarter of delegates from attending.[14] At the 2000 IMF/World Bank meetings in Prague, too, protesters significantly disrupted proceedings.

The media coverage of such protests created the space for establishment figures to break ranks. The most high-profile instance of this came in 2002 when Joseph Stiglitz – a former chief economist of the World Bank – wrote an insider's view of how the policies of the Bretton Woods institutions were contributing to the poverty of nations in the Global South. *Globalization and its Discontents* became an international bestseller and helped explain to those who had remained skeptical what was going wrong.

While Stiglitz's book exposed the errors of a number of politicians and bureaucrats, it was the Canadian author Naomi Klein's book *No Logo* that explained a systemic critique from the ground – arguing that not only workers but consumers too were being exploited by corporate capitalism. In the final section of her book, she celebrates the various strands of resistance, in so doing bringing understanding of the protests to a much wider audience.

As campaigning continued apace across the world, campaigners began to see their actions no longer as isolated campaigns but as part of a global struggle against corporate dominance. At the newly established World Social Forum (formed as a social movement alternative to the World Economic Forum) ideas were exchanged, networks strengthened and co-ordinated days of action decided upon. People retold one another's stories, serving to inspire others. Some attained the status of legends.

In South Africa, the ANC government elected in 1994 had initially proposed social democratic policies, but had come to believe that in the context of globalization it had no choice but to follow the neoliberal path.[15] When it privatized the electricity supply of Soweto, energy bills rocketed to a level beyond what ordinary people could pay. In response, people took to the same streets as they did during the anti-apartheid struggle, using many of the same slogans and many of the same methods. The campaigns also involved some of the same people, including Trevor Ngwane – at one time an anti-apartheid activist who became an ANC councilor before being suspended from the party because of his opposition to privatization. He was one of the people who helped set up the Soweto Electricity Crisis Committee. When people's energy was cut off for non-payment, they moved in to reconnect it illegally. When the Committee was condemned by the authorities, it cut off the electricity supplies to politicians' houses instead. The movement subsequently joined with others to grow into the countrywide Anti-Privatization Forum.[16]

In another resonant episode, following an economic crisis caused by a decade of neoliberal rule, Argentineans filled the streets in December 2001 pounding pots and pans chanting *Que se vayan todos* – 'everyone must go'. Supermarkets were looted to feed the poor, traffic was blocked, banks were smashed and popular assemblies formed. The President who had brought economic ruin to the country by embracing the programs of the IMF was forced to resign, and the country then got through three more presidents in the following 12 days. Nearly 200 abandoned factories were occupied by their workers and run as democratic co-operatives.[17] According to a March 2002 newspaper poll, 50 per cent of people in Buenos Aires saw the neighborhood assemblies as a viable way of governing.[18]

In Bolivia, a people's uprising took place over the early 2000s in response to plans to sell the country's entire water supply to the US corporation Bechtel – as 'suggested' by the World Bank. People faced price hikes of up to $20 in a country where the minimum wage was under $100 a month. Community-run water systems were seized and even collecting rainwater became illegal without a permit. The people's campaign was led by the

Coordinora – a network of community activists supported by the infrastructure of the Cochabamba Federation of Factory Workers.[19]

The protesters began in December 1999 with the Idea Counterpower of demonstrations – to which the government responded by using teargas for the first time in over a decade. Negotiations ensued but, when these broke down, protesters seized control of a central square. The movement also used Economic Counterpower by encouraging people to refuse to pay their bills. When the government still did not give in, the movement employed the Physical Counterpower tactic of an indefinite roadblock to undermine the economic power of the government. Although the state responded by shooting to kill, the sustained campaign led to the revocation of the Bechtel contract. When Bechtel then attempted to sue Bolivia, the continued campaign helped explain to many what was wrong with the neoliberal model. Following a campaign involving a general strike, direct action against banks and the recruiting of police officers to the movement's cause, the President was forced to stand down. In his place anti-neoliberal campaigner Evo Morales was elected as the first indigenous president of the country in 2006.

The early years of the anti-globalization movement certainly built Idea Counterpower. They signaled a rupture with the perceived public consensus for corporate globalization by putting an important set of ideas on the agendas of mainstream academics and commentators, while bringing new attention to the views of those previously considered on the fringes. Through articles, websites and books, the global justice movement built a base of Idea Counterpower that would sustain and inform future mobilizations.

One result of the spotlight the movement shone on corporate misdeeds was the rise of so-called 'Corporate Social Responsibility'. Of course in many cases such initiatives are little more than greenwash, but the movement can take some credit (though many might not wish it) for what limited good they may have done. By targeting businesses such as Starbucks, the movement also created the political space in which church and NGO campaigners could carry the idea of fair trade from the margins to the mainstream. In turn, interest in the reasoning behind fair trade has been a route for many people into the global justice movement.

The Physical Counterpower of direct action also had an effect. The Prague summit was forced to finish a day early, the Seattle WTO meeting was disrupted for a day. At the 2003 WTO talks in Cancún, poor countries walked out altogether, saying that no deal was better than a bad deal that would make them poorer.[20] In many countries of the Global South, Physical Counterpower tactics were merged with the Economic Counterpower of worker-led groups and the Idea Counterpower of a different vision of society to bring about wholesale changes of government. Most notably a swathe of neoliberal regimes were displaced in many countries of Latin America.

With some praiseworthy exceptions, the global justice movement in rich countries did not work closely with the trade union movement. Without the option of the Economic Counterpower of strikes, some activists used the blunter instrument of property damage. It is likely that this helped to undermine the economic power of corporations to some extent, and, more significantly, to damage the idea power of their brands. On the other hand, it may have robbed the movement of some of its potential Idea Counterpower as some people without access to the movement's own media began to associate anti-capitalism only with people smashing things up.

The image of the protesters was not helped by the aggressive actions of the police. The protests of the global justice movement have been amongst the most violently policed demonstrations in the Global North. At most summit protests, activists were met with rubber bullets, teargas, truncheons, shields and horses. In

Geneva, police caused serious injuries to a protester by cutting the rope by which he was hanging off a bridge with a banner.[21] In Gothenburg, police shot three people with live ammunition and also allowed neo-Nazis to attack demonstrators.[22] In Genoa, police engaged in violent raids on protesters' sleeping quarters, abused activists in prison, fabricated evidence in trials, and even shot a man dead – 23-year-old Carlo Giuliani.[23] Such reports are unlikely to have made the movement seem a safe place for people dipping their toes in the water of activism.

Another problematic effect of police tactics was the way that such confrontations were reported. The headline in the British tabloid the *Daily Star* following J18 that screamed 'booze-fuelled hardcore anarchists turn anti-capitalist protest into orgy of violence' was not atypical of the way that demonstrations across the world have been reported. This of course contributed to the idea power of élites which were able to characterize the movement as mindless rioters rather than thoughtful campaigners committed to change.

While the struggles in the Global South continued, the movement in the rich world, as defined by the characteristics of its early phase, began to recede as efforts were diverted towards opposing the preparations of the US and other countries to go to war in Iraq.[24] But the movement did not go away. In fact it was at the 2002 meeting of the World Social Forum that the date was decided for what would become the largest day of action in the history of the world.

The wars in Afghanistan and Iraq

The United States election of 2000 gave a boost to corporations' power. The new President – George W Bush – was a former oil executive. His Vice-President, Dick Cheney, was a former chief executive of the Halliburton corporation. More than 100 former corporate lobbyists were then appointed to positions supposedly responsible for regulating their own industries.[25] In the elections of 2000, 2002 and 2004, 78-80 per cent of party political donations from the oil and gas sector went to the Republicans.[26]

After the al-Qaeda attacks on the World Trade Center towers and the Pentagon on 11 September 2001, the US army invaded Afghanistan and then Iraq – with the support of a number of other countries, including Britain and Australia. Around 3,000 civilians were killed due to the war on Afghanistan[27] – an eerily similar number to those killed on 9/11. More than 100,000 people died due to the invasion of Iraq, despite the absence of a link between that country and al-Qaeda.[28]

Especially in the US and the UK, much of the energy of global justice activists was pulled into the effort to attempt to stop these wars. In some ways it was an obvious transition. Many perceived the real reason for the invasions as the attempt to secure a pipeline, in the case of Afghanistan, and oil reserves in the case of Iraq. The slogan 'No blood for oil' was fully consistent with the earlier protests against rich countries and corporations using their physical and economic muscle to force developing countries to open up their markets. But they were not alone. Within three days of the 9/11 attacks, a number of left-oriented groups in the US formed a new organization: the A.N.S.W.E.R. Coalition (Act Now Stop War End Racism). Its first large protest on 25 September brought 40,000 people on to the streets of San Francisco and Washington DC.[29] Another coalition that formed was United for Peace and Justice – including in its ranks Peace Action, the American Friends Service Committee and the National Council of Churches. In Australia and Britain, the largest organizations adopted the name 'Stop the War Coalition'. For some activists in the global justice movement who had become accustomed to flatter forms of organization, working within these hierarchically structured coalitions was an uneasy fit.

They had a job on their hands to persuade populations of the case against war. Widespread shock at the events of 9/11 stimulated a belief that 'something had to be done'. The phrase

'The War on Terror' was coined by the US government and used widely in news reports. Bush's approval ratings rocketed to 90 per cent. Reports circulated that a number of anti-war songs had been removed from the playlists of commercial radio stations owned by the Clear Channel Corporation.[30] In the Senate, the authorization of the use of force against Afghanistan won unanimous support from Democrats and Republicans. In the House Of Representatives, 420 politicians voted for the use of force with only one representative voting against. In Britain, Labour Prime Minister Tony Blair gave his full support to the invasion of Afghanistan, as did the leadership of the Conservatives and Liberal Democrats.

In the time that followed, a battle of ideas raged. On one side were the pro-war government representatives, corporate spokespeople and military officials who offered the 'expert' analysis in much of the media. On the other was the anti-war movement. Through the Idea Counterpower of alternative media channels like the US radio program *Democracy Now*, public meetings, demonstrations, stunts and straightforward persuasion in the streets at vigils and stalls, the movement slowly won support for its cause. One by one, the anti-war movement countered the arguments for war. In 2002, around 23 Senators and 133 Representatives voted against the war in Iraq – many more than the number who voted against the invasion of Afghanistan. But the idea power of the US government remained too strong.

The peak of the Co-ordination Stage of the anti-war campaign came on 15 February 2003. Participants in the World Social Forum had agreed some months previously that this date would be a day of global protest against the war. The event was bigger than anyone could have imagined. Three million marched in Italy, 1.5 million in England,[31] 1.3 million in Spain, 500,000 in Australia and 75,000 in Scotland. In the US, there were protests in 150 different cities. Even in countries such as France and Germany, whose governments had refused to participate in the war, hundreds of thousands of people marched. In total, there were protests in 60 countries with as many as 10 million people taking part across the world.[32] The *New York Times* declared that there were now two superpowers: the US government and global public opinion.[33]

The polls that followed showed that the balance was indeed beginning to tip. In Britain, opposition to the war broke through the 50-per-cent mark on 18 February 2003 – just three days after the mass marches. Tony Blair's personal approval rating plummeted to minus 20. And still the anti-war demonstrations continued. This had an effect on some politicians in the House of Commons. On 18 March 2003, 149 UK MPs voted against committing troops to Iraq. It was the biggest parliamentary rebellion of Labour's time in office. But it wasn't enough.

The day that war broke out was dubbed 'Day X' by protesters.[34] In Spain, up to 50,000 school and university students took to the streets. In Italy, there were more than 85 strikes, protests and sit-ins. In Seattle, 8,000 students from 30 colleges walked out on strike. Elsewhere in the US, a non-hierarchical network called Direct Action to Stop the War organized the occupation of the financial district of San Francisco, disruptions at military recruitment centers and blocked traffic in major cities. In Britain, students from at least 50 schools left their classrooms and a number of workers took the afternoon off to protest in city centers. The day before war broke out, two activists pulled off an even more audacious act. They broke into Fairford airbase in Gloucestershire to damage the B-52 jets which were imminently to be used in a war illegal under international law.[35] It was the beginning of the Confrontation Stage.

Despite the events of 'Day X', civil disobedience did not become a sustained mainstream movement tactic. Instead, many activists put their effort into electoral organizing. In Spain the strategy saw notable success. A national election after the war had begun gave campaigners a focus and forced an electoral confrontation. The mass demonstrations had been an important factor in changing public opinion. Another factor was a political bombing in the country which highlighted for many how the government's support for the war had made Spain a target. Unlike the US and Britain, where both major parties supported the war, the Spanish movement was boosted by the anti-war stance of the main opposition party. Come the elections, the pro-war Partido Popular was swept from office and the country changed its policy. As soon as possible thereafter, Spain withdrew its troops from Iraq.

In Britain, the successes were more moderate. It is nevertheless testament to the Idea Counterpower accrued by the movement that television pundits predicting a 'Baghdad Bounce' for Labour in the 2003 local and regional elections were forced to eat their words when anti-war parties advanced at the expense of supporters of the invasion. This was most clear in Scotland where the Scottish Socialist Party and Scottish Green Party increased their representation in the Scottish Parliament from one seat each to six and seven respectively. Then, in the General Election of 2005, a new anti-war party, RESPECT, became the first left-of-Labour party to have an MP elected to the House of Commons for 50 years when it overturned a 10,000 strong Labour majority in the London constituency of Bethnal Green and Bow.[36]

In the US, too, much of the effort turned to driving George Bush from office. This was assisted by a torrent of effective uses of Idea Counterpower. Michael Moore's film *Fahrenheit 9/11* became the highest-grossing documentary of all time. 'Netroots' bloggers bloomed in popularity. Online platforms such as Moveon.org extended their reach. Country-music group The Dixie Chicks fought off a wave of criticism for having said that they were ashamed that President Bush came from their home state of Texas. Punk bands including NOFX, Green Day, Anti-Flag and The Offspring organized rock concerts and compilation albums against Bush. In local government there were more than 160 symbolic anti-war motions passed condemning the government's policy – proving that being against war did not mean losing votes.[33] In 2005, a majority of the US public finally turned against the war.[37]

An important factor in the change in public opinion was an act of civil disobedience by Cindy Sheehan – a mother from California whose son had been killed in Iraq. When she camped outside George Bush's window, demanding that the President met her to answer her questions, hundreds joined her and it was covered by the nation's press. Yet, when Sheehan criticized the Democratic Party for voting to fund the war, she became subject to attacks from some of those who had previously praised her.

One of the actions of anti-war activists within the Democratic Party was to help build support for a little known Senator who had spoken against the war at a rally in 2002 – Barack Obama. After a long campaign he won both the Democratic nomination and the presidential election of 2008. That this was a step forward for liberal politics in the US is not in doubt. But whether this was in the end a success for the peace movement is open to question. On the campaign trail in 2007, Obama declared: 'I will promise you this: if we have not gotten our troops out by the time I am president, it is the first thing I will do.'[38] Yet, at the time of writing, two-and-a-half years after Obama became president, US troops are still involved in Iraq and Afghanistan – and now in Libya too.

By the time the campaign reached the Consolidation Stage it was clear that it had not succeeded in stopping the war. The movement used its Idea Counterpower to win the argument, but despite demonstration turnouts comparable to those against the war in Vietnam, the movement did not succeed in translating that strength of feeling into sufficient Economic Counterpower or Physical Counterpower to win the campaign. As Tom Hayden (himself an activist turned politician) advised in 2007, in order to stop the war 'the voters have to threaten the status quo, not just vote against it'.[33]

One country where anti-war protests *did* threaten the

status quo was Egypt, where the campaign sowed the seeds of revolution less than 10 years later – as the next chapter will show. The gains in most countries were on a somewhat smaller scale, but almost everywhere the campaign resulted in significant numbers of people becoming politically active for the first time. Helping to organize the school and college walkouts was, for many young people, a first experience of collective dissent. And the next opportunity to continue the struggle was not far away. In 2005, leaders of eight of the world's richest countries gathered in Scotland for the G8. The movement was there to meet them.

The struggle against global poverty

While the focus of many in rich countries turned to anti-war activism, the campaigns in the Global South against the poverty-inducing effects of the international finance institutions continued apace. In the year 2002 alone, the World Development Movement charted 111 protests in 25 poor countries, with millions of participants in total.[39] The majority of these protests were targeted against the policies of the World Bank and IMF. Many were repressed with physical power, which led to thousands of injuries and arrests and 10 documented deaths.

Especially since 1999, the institutions of global economic power had gone from being obscure acronyms to being hotly discussed topics. The protests planted the germ of an idea in the public consciousness: that the 'free' market policies which the world's corporations said would work for everyone, clearly weren't working for everyone and that the rules of world trade were benefiting the rich at the expense of the poor. Even the supposedly benign arena of international aid came in for criticism as it emerged that, in some cases, official aid was being used to incentivize the sale of public services to corporations from donor countries.

A new issue had been placed on the agenda – an issue in need of a name. At the same time, mainstream media reports of the protests pigeon-holed anti-corporate campaigners as violent rioters. A brainstorm in the offices of the British student campaign group People & Planet sought to address this, and came up with a new term: 'trade justice'. This was a powerful tool for spreading critical consciousness. No longer was the status quo referred to as 'free trade' but as trade *in*justice. No longer were campaigners defined by what they were against, but they had a new way of expressing what they were for.

Until that point, the campaigns of development NGOs had largely focused on the issues of debt cancellation and maintaining development aid. People & Planet campaigner Guy Hughes sought to change this by contacting a number of NGOs and faith groups to discuss organizing a new coalition around trade justice.[40] They were keen. And so the Trade Justice Movement was born – a broad alliance committed to public communications, research and lobbying on the details of the structures and institutions of the global economic system.

NGOs in the Trade Justice Movement and the Jubilee Debt Campaign (successor to Jubilee 2000) were among the organizations that began meeting with Comic Relief co-founder Richard Curtis to start planning for the 2005 G8 Summit. In 2004, a meeting of social movements took place in Johannesburg as a step to a new alliance being launched at the World Social Forum. It had a single focus: poverty. This international alliance called itself the Global Call to Action against Poverty, or GCAP for short. National-level alliances in Canada, Australia and Britain adopted the name 'Make Poverty History'. The US chapter adopted the name 'ONE', with 'the campaign to make poverty history' as its tagline.

In the 2005 G8 host country of Britain, the 500 NGOs that constituted the Make Poverty History alliance sought to communicate one central message: 'Justice not Charity'. They agreed on three central demands: trade justice, drop the debt, more and better aid. They chose to use just one method: Idea Counterpower. Borrowing marketing methods from the private sector (even the name was recommended by an advertising company) the alliances took Idea Counterpower to heights never before seen in the anti-poverty movement.

The campaign was launched in January 2005, when it arranged for a specially scripted sitcom to be shown on national television. This was followed in February by a vigil for trade justice in Trafalgar Square at which Nelson Mandela was a speaker. He declared: 'Like slavery and apartheid, poverty is not natural. It is man-made and it can be overcome and eradicated by the actions of human beings'. He praised the campaign for trade justice, calling it 'a truly meaningful way for the developed countries to show commitment to bringing about an end to global poverty' and finished with some inspiring words: 'Sometimes it falls upon a generation to be great. You can be that great generation. Let your greatness blossom.'[41]

Following this, various celebrities appeared on television clicking their fingers to represent the child that dies every three seconds from extreme poverty. Millions of people wore white bands, ostensibly to show their support for the campaign. Then, the Saturday before the G8 was due to meet, nearly a quarter of a million people took to the streets of Edinburgh, forming a mass white band around the city center, culminating in a rally on the Meadows. It was one of the largest demonstrations in Scottish history.

The Idea Counterpower of the movement which was built up through the Consciousness and Co-ordination stages was impressive. According to opinion polls, the proportion of people in the UK who said they were concerned about global poverty rose to 73 per cent in 2005.[42] The number of people who said they were 'very concerned' rose to 32 per cent, having been around 25 per cent since 1997.[43]

To the consternation of some activists, the same government against which many people were campaigning had an apparent enthusiasm for Make Poverty History. A level of skepticism was voiced when the (then) minister for international development Hilary Benn joined the Make Poverty History march through

Edinburgh. As George Monbiot mused in a newspaper column: 'What would he be chanting – "down with me and all I stand for?".[44] He was right to be concerned.

While Make Poverty History was being built, another initiative was being constructed in parallel – this one altogether closer to the government's agenda. It was called 'Live 8' – a series of concerts in direct competition for attendance and attention with the Make Poverty History march. The person who brought it together was former Boomtown Rats singer Bob Geldof – a known associate of Blair and a member of his 'Commission for Africa'.

A 2010 study of whether Make Poverty History was successful in communicating the 'Justice not Charity' message concluded that, for the wider public at least, it was not. A major reason for this was that Live 8 and Make Poverty History had become intermingled in the public eye. The very name 'Live 8' reinforced memories of the 1985 charity concerts 'Live Aid'. As a result, the movement was perceived most widely as calling for rich countries to give more money to poor countries rather than as a movement for the transformation of power.[43]

The prominence of Live 8 presented another problem: Bob Geldof's high profile meant that he was perceived by the general public as the spokesperson for the movement as a whole. When Geldof declared that the G8 had delivered 'ten out of ten on aid, eight out of ten on debt' his words caused outrage amongst the many anti-poverty campaigners who concurred with the view of GCAP chair Kumi Naidoo: 'The people have roared but the G8 has whispered.'[45]

Not everyone was in a mood to ask the G8 to be a little nicer. Some campaigners argued that the best way to make poverty history would be to abolish the G8 altogether. Two more radical alliances were formed in addition to Make Poverty History. The first was 'Dissent!' – an international network with its roots in the anti-globalization movement. The second was 'G8 Alternatives' – a group with a membership and structure not dissimilar to the Stop the War Coalition.

On the day of the summit itself, the G8 Alternatives grouping marched on Gleneagles gate while Dissent! blocked roads around the venue. The G8 Alternatives march included banners from, amongst others, War on Want, the Campaign for Nuclear Disarmament and a number of green and socialist parties. The placards were in four languages reading 'another world is possible'. The police blocked off the front of the march then charged the crowds. People covered their heads and were crushed closer together as no way to move became apparent. Some way along, a breach in the outer perimeter fence had been made. People streamed through it as the media recorded them. Before long a Chinook helicopter landed, out of which came police with batons and dogs who beat the protesters back. Whether intentional or not, Conscientization and Co-ordination had turned to Confrontation. But what little power the movement had was crushed by physical force and the idea power of skilful government PR.

The Consolidation Stage that followed revealed that there was, in fact, progress. Although debt cancellation was only offered to 19 highly indebted poor countries, there are, nevertheless, people today with access to school and healthcare who would not otherwise have had that access.[46] Although the IMF continued to insist on neoliberal conditions to debt relief, including the selling of public services to corporations, campaign groups were able to capitalize on the high profile of the issues and wrench a promise from the British government to stop attaching neoliberal conditionalities to direct aid.[47] And although the G8 reneged on its aid pledge,[48] successive governments in Britain have increased their international development budgets, citing Make Poverty History as one of their reasons for doing so.

However, the success of campaigns cannot only be measured by progress against stated objectives. The beauty of mass campaigns is that new ideas and networks emerge which protest organizers could never have predicted. The campaigns around the 2005 G8 brought another influx of people into campaigning and informed them about global injustice and corporate power – for example, in the week following the mass march, a number of the more radical organizations in the Make Poverty History alliance put on a mass conference entitled 'Corporate G8'.[49] And for the week of the G8 many activists in the Dissent! network stayed on a convergence campsite where relationships were built that would reshape radical campaigning for at least the following five years.

The fight against climate change

Awareness of the problems associated with fossil-fuel extraction grew through the 1990s and 2000s. In 1993, Bill Clinton and Al Gore were elected President and Vice-President of the United States, pledging to cut CO_2 emissions. But even though they recruited prominent environmentalists into their government, many of their ambitions were dropped.[50] By the time Clinton stood down as President, CO_2 emissions in the US had risen by 18 per cent.[51]

In Nigeria, thousands of people took part in campaigns against the environmental degradation caused by Shell in the Niger Delta.[52] In 1995, Ken Saro-Wiwa and eight other campaigners in Nigeria were killed by the state. His name became known around the world. It also focused attention on Shell – widely believed to have been implicated in his fate. Another prominent international speaker on the issue today has been Friends of the Earth International chair Nnimmo Bassey. In his view, the struggle against resource colonialism in Nigeria has been fought for over 100 years. As he explains: 'It was in 1895 that the first Nigerian people were massacred for access to palm oil. Now, over a century later – there has been no change, except now it's crude oil'.[53]

Campaigning by green groups led to the Kyoto Protocol on global warming being adopted in 1997. However, following lobbying by corporations (including an anti-Kyoto television advertising campaign costing $23 million[51]) a series of market-based loopholes were inserted, including a mechanism for rich countries to 'buy' greenhouse-gas reductions from poor countries. Even then the overall target was wholly inadequate, as it was agreed to cut CO_2 by just 5.2 per cent below 1990 levels by 2012.

Just a month after the Prague protests in 2000, a network of groups under the banner 'Rising Tide' met at the sixth Conference of Parties (CoP) Summit in The Hague. Having read the policy reports of the NGOs and followed the previous CoP summits, many had concluded that the only chance for achieving the CO_2 cuts necessary to avoid the worst effects of climate change would be a transformation to a post-capitalist society – the very antithesis of what was on the table at CoP6, labeled by one activist 'a trade fair poorly disguised as an environmental conference'.[54]

The most audacious act of The Hague week of action was when activists forged passes and entered the talks themselves. They dropped banners, disrupted meetings, and even put a pie in the face of US negotiator Frank E Loy. They were condemned both by government delegates and by many NGOs. But their pre-emptive act of confrontation set in train a series of events that would shape the climate movement.

In the years that followed, climate change campaigning steadily grew, but was often overshadowed by other headline concerns. The turning-point for many activists came in 2005. One of the spaces the international Dissent! network set up during the 2005 G8 mobilization was a purpose-built non-hierarchical eco-village consciously designed to create a space for anti-capitalists and environmentalists to meet and share ideas. Many of the younger activists there were students, politicized by the protests against the Iraq war, staying in the area of the camp organized by People & Planet. At daily consensus-based meetings, they rubbed shoulders with direct-action old hands from across the world, many of whom were veterans of Rising Tide, Reclaim the Streets, Earth First! and anarchist groups.

The result was momentous. The camp could be seen as the peak of the Consciousness Stage, with the growing feeling that, rather than primarily focusing on international summits, efforts might be better spent tackling the problem of climate change at source. This was quickly followed by the early Co-ordination Stage when the decision was made to form the first Camp for Climate Action – colloquially known as the Climate Camp.

The Climate Camp concept rolls in to one the main characteristics of a training camp: autonomous space and sustainable community. Most importantly, the focus is action – either there or thereafter. The first Climate Camp took place in summer 2006 on land close to a coal-fired power station owned by E.ON. In the years that followed, Climate Camps – or their equivalents – were established in countries including Wales, Scotland, Ireland, the US, Canada, Denmark, Sweden, Switzerland, France, Germany, Belgium, India, New Zealand, Australia, Ghana and Ukraine.[55]

Coal formed a particular focus for the movement. For example, at the German *KlimaCamp* in 2008, campaigners joined with local groups in Hamburg to attempt to stop the construction of a power station there. In March 2009, Climate Camp Australia attempted to 'switch off' the Hazelwood coal-fired power station through mass direct action. In June they succeeded in disabling another coal power plant by locking themselves to the conveyor belt. In June 2008, a group in England used safety signals to flag down a coal train then board it, and in 2009 activists successfully scaled a chimney near Oxford. In the same month hundreds of people descended on the Ratcliffe-on-Soar power station in Nottingham to pull down fences and attempt to close it down.

A particular concern for the movement in North America has been Mountain Top Removal (MTR) mining in Appalachia – a process through which the tops of more than 500 mountains have quite literally been blasted off as the quickest way of accessing the coal within, causing significant local pollution in addition to the coal's contribution to global climate change. A number of Mountain Justice summer camps organized by academics, local campaigners and members of Rising Tide and Earth First! brought in new activists from across the country – especially students – to lend their solidarity to long-running community campaigns.

Actions flowing out of the camps have included office occupations, power station blockades, demonstrations, stunts and lock-ons, including by NASA scientist James Hansen, who has been arrested on a number of occasions as part of the campaign. Although MTR mining has not been halted, the campaign did see a success when the authorities responded to pressure by agreeing to provide a new school for children in the area whose previous building had been close to a slurry impoundment.[56]

In the UK, the movement saw its greatest successes when it linked up with existing community campaigns. In 2007 the Climate Camp targeted Heathrow Airport[57] and in 2008 the coal-fired power station at Kingsnorth in Kent. As part of a wider campaign, plans for a third runway at Heathrow and a new power station at Kingsnorth were eventually shelved.[58]

The Climate Camp has suffered physical repression throughout its life – typified by events at the 2008 Kingsnorth camp. Police deprived campaigners of sleep at night by playing loud music, including Wagner. There were illegal stop-and-searches at the entrance and police raids on the camp. When two female activists pointed out that police were not wearing their numbers they were bundled to the ground and held in custody for four days.[59] This came alongside a media attack carrying a story that 70 police had been hurt at the camp. It later transpired that the sources of injury included toothache, diarrhoea, cut fingers and even 'possible bee stings'.[60] Through a sustained and skilful media operation, the Climate Camp slowly began to debunk the myths and win the sympathy of many mainstream media sources.

At the same time as Climate Camp was being formed,

relationships between organizations involved in the Make Poverty History campaign were a factor in the creation of a new coalition. Anti-poverty NGOs joined with their green counterparts, pointing out that climate change could make poverty permanent. Stop Climate Chaos was formed in September 2005. In Canada and Australia, Make Poverty History platforms kept their name but made action on climate change a top-line demand.

Possibly the biggest success of the Stop Climate Chaos coalition was the campaign spearheaded by Friends of the Earth to persuade the British government to pass the world's first Climate Change Act, enshrining in law targets to reduce CO_2 by 80 per cent by 2050. Against all odds, the Bill was proposed and, one by one, loopholes that would have excluded emissions from aviation and shipping were closed. The passing of the Act was momentous and groundbreaking. Unfortunately, due to lobbying by corporations, one loophole remained. The bill allowed the UK to 'offset' its CO_2 emissions by paying those in other countries to emit less carbon. Despite the evidence that such market mechanisms are unlikely to stop climate change,[61] such instruments remain central to the negotiating position of many rich countries at international summits.

One of the most respected opponents of such 'false solutions' is the Indian activist Vandana Shiva. In her book *Soil Not Oil* she explains how carbon offsets burden the poor twice – 'first with the externalized costs and climate disasters caused by the pollution of others and then with the burden of remediating the pollution of the rich and powerful'. She is equally derisive of carbon trading, which 'allows polluters to keep polluting' while 'economic actors that never polluted were never allocated credits and therefore are never able to sell them. There is nothing to encourage truly sustainable development'.[62]

Protests against market mechanisms had long been a feature of the movement in the Global South. In 2002, for example, the Soweto Electricity Crisis Committee helped organize a

30,000-strong demonstration in conjunction with the World Summit on Sustainable Development in Durban, which they dubbed the 'W$$D'. In Latin America, La Via Campesina has also been outspoken in its opposition to systems that would both further harm the poor and fail to solve the problem.

The Climate Camp began to emphasize the problems with carbon trading in 2009, when 5,000 people protested outside the European Climate Exchange to coincide with the G20 Summit taking place in London. A festival-like atmosphere was brought to a busy street in the financial district of London, succeeding in closing it off to cars completely. As with Reclaim the Streets, there were samba bands and sound systems. Unlike previous protests there was also a Scottish ceilidh. Some of the Climate Campers set up tents and pledged to stay the night. The police had other ideas. In the early evening they 'kettled' protesters (corralling them together – later ruled illegal), and hit them with batons.[63] At a parallel protest on a nearby street a man died after having been struck by a police officer.

The 2009 Conference of the Parties Summit in Copenhagen was billed by some as the conference that could make a deal that would save the world. Stop Climate Chaos agreed with its international counterparts to argue for a fair, ambitious and binding climate deal. Across the world, 17 million people took action to support the call – although many of these were online petitions.[64] Shortly before the start of the talks, 50,000 people took to the streets of London – breaking records as the biggest march against climate change ever, only to be trumped on the streets of Copenhagen itself a few days later.

The process inside the conference center was comparable to trade negotiations. According to the negotiator for the G77 group of poor countries, rich nations were guilty of bullying, bribery and backroom deals to try to bring about an arrangement that would still further advance the interests of the rich at the expense of the poor.[65] Proposals on the table in line with the science were sidelined. As it became abundantly clear that no climate-protecting deal would be made by the parties to the official negotiations, activists from a number of social movements marched to the site of the talks and attempted to breach the fence with the aim of holding their own 'People's Assembly' in the grounds, to make the case for the solutions that had been frozen out of the official process. As they did so, a number of delegates from inside the conference center marched out to meet them. Both groups were violently repressed by the Danish police.

Those who had hoped for a fair, ambitious, binding deal at Copenhagen were disappointed. Many veterans of trade summits had never expected that it would. A positive factor to come out of the mobilization, however, was the way that activists met with counterparts from across the world, laying the foundations for a civil society conference a year later in the Bolivian city of Cochabamba aimed at organizing a way of winning Climate Justice with or without the discredited CoP process.[66]

The increased Idea Counterpower of the climate change movement can be seen in the way that rhetoric about global warming has been lifted from a marginal concern to the top of the public and political agenda and, to some extent, in the election of Green parliamentarians. But there is a question as to whether the movement has succeeded in communicating the necessity of a different economic system in order to deliver a safe climate. Even the actions of the explicitly anti-capitalist Climate Camps were interpreted by many as calls for carbon cuts in isolation rather than demands for a radically different economic system.[67] In the face of calls for renewed action on climate change on the one hand and lobbying from business groups to maintain the current system on the other, policy-makers turned to the path of least resistance: unworkable market-based non-solutions.

There has been a substantial amount of Physical Counterpower organized. But despite some notable actions, the biggest Climate Camps attracted only a few thousand people and a still smaller number of those felt able to take part in arrestable direct action.

This is far from the scale that won change in campaigns past, even though the urgency of climate change makes this issue arguably more important than any other.

As with the other campaigns of the global justice movement, the climate change movement has struggled to utilize Economic Counterpower. Boycotts – for example of oil corporations – have on the whole been designed as methods of Idea Counterpower rather than as serious attempts to damage profits. The notion of the green ban as applied to climate change remains underutilized. There has been some co-operation with workers – including a significant campaign in solidarity with wind turbine makers on the Isle of Wight who occupied their factory when it was threatened with closure. However, such actions have remained the exception rather than the rule – and even the example cited amounted more to Physical Counterpower than Economic Counterpower. Having said that, trade unions have begun to speak of the need for a 'just transition'. If these words are developed into Economic Counterpower, the green cause might find a new, potentially effective method of resistance.

As I write, the climate movement rolls on. Literally as I type these words, an email has popped up on my screen telling me of an action in Washington DC involving hundreds of people occupying the offices of the Department of the Interior in protest at indigenous and public land being leased to coal and oil corporations. As I come back to edit, I have another email in my inbox telling me that people in many countries have taken action against BP to coincide with their AGM, especially to protest the extraction of oil from tar sands in Alberta, Canada.

But by now yet another front of protest has opened up.

The financial crisis and its impacts

In 2008, the world experienced a financial crisis born of greed, complacency and a disastrous set of government policies that allowed banking corporations more and more power. Following the largest bank bailout in history, recession and reduced tax receipts, 2010 brought government-enforced austerity, rising unemployment and an increase in inequality. In some ways the global justice movement is returning to its foundations in resisting structural adjustment. The difference is that now it isn't just happening in poor countries, but in rich countries as well.

There has also been a new resurgence in summit protests – as familiar alliances have organized major mobilizations to coincide with the G20 summits in London, Pittsburgh, Toronto and Seoul. The protests have not been confined to summits, though, and in Greece, France, Britain and the US, to name just four countries, campaigns against the effects of neoliberal economics have contained a significant direct-action component.

In late 2010, a group of campaigners, many whom knew each other through Climate Camp, met in a North London pub to discuss their response. On the table was a copy of the magazine *Private Eye* that included an article saying that Vodafone had dodged six billion pounds in tax – not dissimilar to the amount that the finance minister George Osborne would soon slash from the welfare budget. The group decided to take power into their own hands and occupy Vodafone's flagship store. On 27 October 2010, that is exactly what they did.

The action had an overwhelmingly positive response, from passers-by, from the mainstream press (even some of those who do not traditionally support such things), and, importantly, on the social media networks of the internet. The idea went viral. Publicized via Facebook, Twitter and the friendship networks of Climate Camp and other activist organizations, almost 30 Vodafone stores were occupied the following Saturday. As the protests went on, the attention shifted to other tax-dodging shops, then to the banks that had either dodged tax or caused the crisis. Soon US Uncut was established, along with Canada Uncut and France Uncut.

A statement on the UK Uncut website embodies the principles of Counterpower: 'Austerity-economics is the policy of the powerful. It cannot be stopped by asking nicely. We cannot wait until the next election. If we want to win the fight against these cuts (and we can win) then we must make it impossible to ignore our arguments and impossible to resist our demands.'[68] The latest manifestation of the global justice movement is happening now on the streets, in the media and on the internet. Buoyed by the experience of the recent past, the anti-cuts campaign is already more widespread and more militant than any campaign of the recent past.

But it is in North Africa that protests against the effects of neoliberalism have gone the furthest – even leading to the downfall of presidents. It is to the revolution in Egypt that the next chapter will turn.

1 Institute for Policy Studies, *The Rise of Corporate Global Power*, nin.tl/ILT0Uk
2 A Zapatista slogan used as the title of Paul Kingsnorth's inspiring and influential book *One No Many Yeses: A Journey to the Heart of the Global Resistance Movement*, Free Press, London, 2003. **3** This is my characterization of the options discussed in Derek Wall, *Babylon and Beyond: the Economics of Anti-Globalist, Anti-Capitalist and Radical Green Movements*, Pluto, London, 2005. **4** Susan George, 'How to Win the War of Ideas: Lessons from the Gramscian Right', *Dissent*, Summer 1997.
5 Naomi Klein, *The Shock Doctrine*, Allen Lane, Toronto, 2007. **6** World Development Movement, *Out of Time: The Case for Replacing the World Bank and IMF*, London, 2006. **7** See Ha-Joon Chang, *Bad Samaritans*, Random House, London, 2007. **8** Amory Starr, *Global Revolt: A Guide to the Movements against Globalization*, Zed, London, 2005. **9** Jubilee Debt Campaign, *Origins of the Debt Movement*, nin.tl/kc91ll **10** 'The Emergence of a Global Movement', Dissent! daysofdissent.org.uk/global.htm **11** Janet Thomas, *The Battle in Seattle: the Story Behind and Beyond the WTO Demonstrations*, Fulcrum, 2000. **12** *Battle in Seattle*, Insight Film Studios, 1999. Some aspects of the film are contested, see David and Rebecca Solnit *The Battle of the Story of the Battle of Seattle*, AK Press, Edinburgh, 2009 **13** Kingsnorth, op cit. **14** *New York Times*, 'Economic Talks Open Minus 200 Delegates: Demonstrators Harass Melbourne Conference', nin.tl/jTopp0 **15** An interview in Paul Kingsnorth's book *One No Many Yeses* makes this particularly clear. **16** Trevor Ngwane and Patrick Bond in Kolya Abramsky (ed), *Sparking a World-wide Energy Revolution – Social Struggles in the Transition to a Post-Petrol World*, AK Press, Oakland, 2009. **17** The documentary film *The Take* by Naomi Klein and Avi Lewis tells the story of some of the worker co-ops. **18** Naomi Klein, 'Elections vs. Democracy in Argentina', nin.tl/kHTIVk **19** See Marcia López Levy, 'The Damn Water is Ours!', *New Internationalist*, Sep 2001 nin.tl/ILU03l
20 Fatoumata Jawara and Aileen Kwa, *Behind the scenes at the WTO*, London: Zed, London, 2003. **21** Indymedia, 'G8 Protests in Evian', nin.tl/muTvX7 **22** 'A Recipe for Repression', Dissent! daysofdissent.org.uk/gothenburg.htm **23** Sources for these: first-hand account of a raid Kingsnorth, op cit; Amnesty International, nin.tl/jcGilY; BBC news, nin.tl/IG2HC2 ; Haidi Giuliani, *Genoa 2001*, in Gill Hubbard and David

Miller (eds) *Arguments against G8*, Pluto, 2005. **24** Some see the last Reclaim the Streets party at the DSEi arms fair in 2003 as the conclusion of the first phase of the global justice movement as defined by its early form. **25** 'When advocates become regulators', *Denver Post*, 23 May 2004. **26** Open Secrets, 'Top Industries', nin.tl/ketfv4 **27** Afghanistan Casualty Count nin.tl/kN1l9H **28** iraqbodycount.org **29** ANSWER Coalition, nin.tl/mDQLIc **30** These included John Lennon's *Imagine*, Edwin Starr's *War* and the entire Rage Against the Machine back catalog. The company denied the existence of such a list. **31** A Guardian/ICM poll showed that at least one person from 1.25 million households in Britain went on the anti-war march in London, confirming estimates that between 1.5 and two million people attended. **32** BBC news, 'Millions join anti-war protests', nin.tl/jUEl8M **33** Tom Hayden, *Ending the War in Iraq*, Akashic, 2007. **34** There was in fact more than one 'Day X' – the first, pre-organized one on 5 March, the second on 19 March as war broke out. 'Day X' was also a name used by a new wave of protesting school students in the British anti-cuts movement eight years later. **35** The campaigners were told to expect a five- to ten-year prison sentence but the 12 jury members found them not guilty. **36** In 1945, two Communist MPs were returned to the British Parliament, including Willie Gallacher of Red Clydeside fame. Before that, a small party named Commonwealth was briefly represented at Westminster. The RESPECT result was the more remarkable in the context of a sustained smear campaign against party leader George Galloway – falsely accused by the *Telegraph* and *Christian Science Monitor* of having taken money from the former Iraqi regime. **37** AEI, *Public Opinion on the War in Iraq*, nin.tl/l0hNY2 **38** Obama campaign promise, 27 Oct 2007 nin.tl/jG1pma **39** WDM, nin.tl/mK86ob **40** Staff members at the World Development Movement and Christian Aid were particularly central. **41** makepovertyhistory.org/extras/mandela.shtml **42** Department for National Statistics, *Public Attitudes Towards Development*, nin.tl/ixXD5k **43** Andrew Darnton and Martin Kirk, *Finding Frames*, Bond, nin.tl/me9tcb **44** George Monbiot, 'The Corporate Continent', 9 Jul 2005, nin.tl/iMz3nn **45** BBC news, 'G8 leaders agree $50 billion aid boost', nin.tl/msuucE **46** Eurodad, 'G8 Debt Deal One Year On', nin.tl/iLaFcJ **47** Oneworld.net, 'UK company's Tanzanian bid fails', nin.tl/jmzlUn **48** Bond, 'G8 Canada 2010', nin.tl/joIL1y **49** Including World Development Movement, War on Want, People and Planet and Friends of the Earth. **50** See John Dryzek *et al* 'The Environmental Transformation of the State: the USA, Norway, Germany and the UK', *Political Studies*, Vol 50, 2002. **51** Danny Chivers, *The No Nonsense Guide to Climate Change*, New Internationalist, Oxford, 2011. **52** For a firsthand account read Ken Saro-Wiwa, *A Month and a Day and Letters*, Ayebia, Banbury, 1996. **53** 6 Billion Ways, 'Africa: From Charity to Resistance', 5 Mar 2011, thetopsoil.org.uk/2011/239 **54** Sam Chase, 'Rising Tide: a Movement for Climate Justice. The Story So Far', in *Socialist Outlook*, 2004. **55** Sophie Cooke, 'Leave it in the Ground – The Growing Global Struggle against Coal' in Kolya Abramsky, *Op Cit* climateconvergence.org and climatecollective.org **56** nin.tl/isRCan **57** For a first-hand account of the Heathrow camp, see Tamsin Omond, *Rush: The making of a climate activist*, Marion Boyars, London, 2009. **58** See John Stewart *Victory Against All Odds*, Hacan, London. **59** *The Guardian*, 'Police at Kingsnorth', nin.tl/k7Kg7U **60** *The Guardian*, 'Minister apologizes for police insect injuries', nin.tl/mhkiba **61** See Sarah-Jayne Clifton, *Offsetting - A Dangerous Distraction*, Friends of the Earth nin.tl/mhXqBa **62** Vandana Shiva, *Soil Not Oil: Climate Change, Peak Oil and Food Insecurity*, Zed, London, 2008. **63** The Climate Camp Legal Team and the crew for the film *Just Do It* have created a video of how the day unfolded, which is online at nin.tl/j7e5l6 **64** GCCA, *Tck Tck Tck*, tcktcktck.org/about-tck/ **65** Bernarditas de Castro Muller, 'Pressure on poor at Copenhagen led to failure, not diplomatic wrangling', http://nin.tl/iHSKwK **66** People's Agreement of Cochabamba, nin.tl/jKf5v6 **67** A perception which the UK camp sought to address by targeting the City of London in 2009 and the Royal Bank of Scotland in 2010. **68** UKUNCUT, nin.tl/kFIDI6

8
How the Egyptians overthrew their president

'You will not be able to stay home, brother. You will not be able to plug in, turn on and cop out.'

Gil Scott-Heron

The events of the 'Arab Spring' have already passed into legend. The story begins on 17 December 2010, in an ordinary town in the center of Tunisia, when a municipal inspector attempted to confiscate fruit from a street vendor by the name of Mohamed Bouazizi. Such occurrences were frequent in the region, where low-paid officials often sought bribes. But Bouazizi didn't have money for a bribe. When he resisted, the inspector slapped him[1] before confiscating his scales – which had been lent to him by a friend. As he didn't have money for new scales, he walked to the municipal building to demand them back. There he was beaten again. Later that day Bouazizi covered himself with paint thinner and set himself on fire.[2]

It was the spark that led to a new wave of dissent. It began later that day when friends and relatives gathered outside the office of the governor. They threw coins, shouting 'here is your bribe'. In the days that followed, more people joined, including trade unionists, even as the police became more repressive. Videos of the protests were posted to the internet, which prompted protests in other cities too. The images struck a chord with people angry at government corruption, the brutality of the police, the lack of jobs and the absence of electoral choice.

After four weeks of protest in which police were repelled and the offices of the ruling party were damaged, President Zine al-Abidine Ben Ali was forced to flee the country. The events inspired activists in Egypt. Even as I write, the struggle in Egypt continues, but the events leading to the downfall of President Mubarak provide an exemplary case study in the use of Counterpower. Idea Counterpower, Economic Counterpower and Physical Counterpower were all used. The principles of escalation and solidarity are clear to be seen. And the movement passed through all the stages of Consciousness, Co-ordination, Confrontation and Consolidation.

Although the autobiographies of the people who made these revolutions happen have not yet been written, much of the story was told online as it happened. Blogs like 3arabwy.org, twitter feeds on the #Jan25 hash tag and satellite television stations such as Al-Jazeera bypassed state media and told the world what was going on.[3] The message that comes through is clear: a new recipe for revolution is emerging. And it is altering the way that the world thinks about social change.

The revolution in Egypt

During the 30 years from 1981 to 2011, Egypt was ruled by Hosni Mubarak. His physical power to put down dissent was propped up by military aid from the US, which by 2011 had reached $1.3 billion a year, widely interpreted as payment for a conciliatory approach to neighboring Israel. The regime's idea power was strengthened through media censorship. Meanwhile a new economic élite with personal or familial ties to the Egyptian regime emerged, often working as junior partners to transnational corporations.[4]

Some journalistic accounts date the beginning of the Egyptian Revolution to 25 January 2011, the day of the first mass protest in Cairo after the fall of the Ben Ali regime in Tunisia. Yet those demonstrations were the result of a movement that had been growing for more than a decade. The Consciousness Stage of the revolution can be traced back to the year 2000, when thousands took to the streets for the first time in decades to protest human rights abuses in Palestine. At first, the protests were only implicitly critical of US influence in the region. But, as activists became bolder, the chants became more explicit. 3arabwy.org blogger Hossam el-Hamalawy recalls that 'the first time I heard protesters *en masse* chanting against the President [was] in April 2002, during the pro-Palestinian riots around Cairo University. Battling the notorious Central Security Forces, protesters were chanting in Arabic: "Hosni Mubarak is just like Sharon".'[5]

When the US and UK invaded Iraq, anti-Mubarak feeling strengthened. More than 30,000 Egyptians faced down police repression to briefly take control of Tahrir Square and even to burn a billboard depicting the President's image. Elements of the anti-war movement then helped lead into the early Co-ordination Stage of the campaign, by organizing a more explicitly pro-democracy movement, within which the most active group was called *Kefaya* ('enough'). It didn't become a truly mass movement, but it did alter Egypt's political culture. Even Egyptians who were not involved became aware of young people in the capital openly defying the regime in a way that had seemed unimaginable only a few years before.

The discontent was heightened by the neoliberal economic programs adopted by the regime, supported by the World Bank and IMF, and enforced through the state's security apparatus. More than half of public-sector factories were sold off. This led to lay-offs of around a third of the workforce in each privatized company, with no apparent gain to the country at large.[4] The most significant instance of this was when the workforce of the textile mill in Mahalla – the biggest in the Middle East – was reduced from 38,000 to 27,000. Women decided to go on strike, calling on the men to join them. When some of their demands were won, they inspired a wave of strikes across the textile sector, then in other sectors of the economy.

On 6 April 2008, another strike was planned. This time it never took place. As the 3arabwy blog read that morning: 'Looks like the strike has been aborted. The company compound is under police siege. The Central Security Forces are surrounding the factory. Most gates have been shut down earlier by the police to control the flow of workers in and out of the factory. Inside the compound, plainclothes security agents are virtually everywhere and are dispersing any crowd of workers who assemble.'[6]

In response, the town erupted with demonstrations, and some activists sought to physically dismantle symbols of the regime. They were fired upon by police. At least three people were killed and hundreds were detained and tortured. The scenes became known as the Mahalla Intifada. In solidarity, a civil engineer named Ahmed Maher set up a Facebook group which rapidly garnered 70,000 members. It was the beginning of what later became known as the April 6 Youth Movement.

Maher and others began meeting, planning and learning – for example, by seeking advice from veterans of the youth-led democracy movement in Serbia. As Maher later explained in an interview for Al-Jazeera: 'Necessity is the mother of invention. If I need to do something, I learn how to do it.' So 'I got training in how to conduct peaceful demonstrations, how to avoid violence and how to face violence from the security forces.'[7] April 6 was only one of a multitude of campaign groups that grew in this time, working for a number of different causes. By 2010, the movement included socialist groups, Kefaya, the April 6 movement and Mohamed El Baradei's Movement for Change.[8]

The economic situation continued to worsen. Food prices rose while wages stayed low. In 2011, the national minimum wage was the same as it had been in 1984: 35 Egyptian pounds a month ($6) – not even enough to buy a bag of tomatoes.[9] Strikes rose to a record high. But it was the success of the Tunisian revolutionaries that provided the impetus to kick-start the next level of struggle. According to student activist Gigi Ibrahim: 'Whenever we called for a protest in Tahrir before, it hadn't happened because the people didn't think it would lead to change... When we saw that the Tunisian people could overthrow a dictator, we began to believe that Egyptians could do it too.'[10]

This was boosted by the use of Twitter and Facebook to bypass the official media channels and get the message out. It was a Facebook group called 'We are all Khaled Said' (a young man widely believed to have been murdered by the police), which had been set up by an Egyptian working abroad and had gathered 100,000 members, that led to the first mass protest on 25 January.

25 January was a national holiday to celebrate the police. As April 6 co-founder Ahmed Maher explains: 'We do this every year but we make fun of it. Every year we distribute pamphlets asking how we can be expected to celebrate these thugs, torturers, criminals. But this year what happened in Tunisia has given a different feel to 25 January.'[11] They had also learned from the repression they had faced previously, and sought to avoid being kettled by organizing 20 different fast-moving processions converging on Tahrir (Liberation) Square. Part of the protest consisted of touring the poor areas chanting slogans related to the economic situation. As the demonstrations picked up numbers, they headed to the town center, overcoming police lines as they went. The police responded with rubber bullets, teargas and water cannons. But the brutality served only to radicalize the movement.

At 7pm a meeting of the social movements took place in Tahrir Square. Gigi Ibrahim was there: 'We said "Now we need to write down what we want", and the main thing we could think of was the arrest of the minister of the interior, who was responsible for many bad things. But the people around us in Tahrir Square, the majority, who didn't belong to any political group, were chanting for the removal of the regime. So we knew at that moment that we couldn't ask for less than the people wanted.'[10] They opted for the more radical demand. Some older activists expressed their skepticism. But, within 18 days, the radical decision was proved to be the right one.

In the days that followed, the regime tried everything it could to suppress the movement, but through escalation and solidarity the protesters stayed resilient. On 28 January – later dubbed 'the Day of Rage' – Mubarak sought simultaneously to co-opt and crush the movement. On the one hand, the President announced the dismissal of his entire cabinet. On the other, the regime ordered police to use brutal force against protesters. But even more people joined the demonstrations on the streets. Hundreds were killed but still the activists held strong. If they were able to do so, people walked upon police lines, chanting 'peaceful protest', hugging police and urging them to change sides and join the revolution. Where that was not possible, the campaigners returned the police fire with stones and teargas canisters, while sheltering behind barricades in the street.

A particular focal point was the event that quickly became known as the Battle of Qasr al-Nil Bridge, during which activists pushed riot police across the bridge that connects Tahrir Square to the upmarket area of Zamalek. Although armed vehicles pursued activists and even ran some of them over, the vehicles were set on fire. Some protesters even attempted to topple a police truck over the edge of the bridge and into the Nile. Similarly confrontational scenes were reported in cities across the country, including protesters seeking to storm buildings and occupy squares, as well as demonstrating in large numbers.[12]

The government sought to reduce the movement's Idea Counterpower by blocking the internet. Yet within a day some citizen journalists began to get back online – by phoning their tweets to friends abroad, using proxies or finding their way on to other servers.

The regime played its next card on 29 January, when it removed the police from the streets entirely, in the hope that public opinion might turn against the movement. Protesters damaged some buildings – mostly institutions associated with the regime such as the governing party's offices, which were set on fire. Citizens' militias were established to keep the peace. As one activist put it on Twitter: 'there is no state at the moment, we're governing ourselves'.

But self-governance did not only belong to the realm of law and order. Tahrir Square itself was effectively a liberated zone autonomously organized through co-operation. Gigi Ibrahim calls it 'a mini-example of what direct democracy looks like. People took charge of everything – trash, food, security. It was a self-sustaining entity. And in the middle of this, under every tent, on every corner, people were having debates about their demands, the future, how things should go economically and politically. It was fascinating. It was a mirror of what Egypt would look like if it was democratic.'[13] And it was something Mubarak's regime was determined to break.

Following a 'million man march' for democracy on 1 February, the regime changed tack. As state media showed calm pictures of the river Nile, and activists got back online, the world learned of events through the tweets of activists in Cairo. At 13.40 on 2 February, 'Sandmonkey' tweeted: '1,000 pro-Mubarak demonstration is heading towards Tahrir. The military is withdrawing. This will get ugly quickly.' Six minutes later 'Travellerw' tweeted: 'Real panic in Tahrir. Square overrun by Mubarak demonstration', then 'Pro-change demo has regrouped and is pushing back the pro-mub demo' before deciding 'fuck reporting. I'm going in'. Within an hour, 'Sandmonkey' quipped: 'Camels and horses used by pro-Mubarak protesters to attack anti-Mubarak protesters. This is becoming literally a circus'. 'Monasosh' wrote: 'Cut wounds, fractures, rupture eyes. Weapons used glass, coke bottles, knives, swords'. As evening fell, Gigi Ibrahim tweeted 'I WILL NOT LEAVE TAHRIR TONIGHT so stop telling me to do so! We need more people in TAHRIR NOW!! Get here for our freedom!!!' Constructing makeshift barricades and using whatever came to hand, the protesters maintained control of the square and repelled the thugs, many of whom turned out to be police. The protesters wrestled a number of police ID cards (later photographed and broadcast via Twitter) from the people who had attacked, while other pro-regime demonstrators admitted that they had been paid to attend.

When Mubarak announced that he would not stand in the next election a new divide in opinion in the movement emerged. Some thought that Mubarak's promise not to stand again was enough. Others demanded the immediate resignation of the President so that he could not change his mind once the movement had subsided. The army began expressing doubts as to whether it could maintain control of the country. The regime was running out of cards to play. But the movement kept finding new opportunities to escalate the struggle.

Soon after returning to Egypt from his work abroad to join the demonstrations, one of the administrators of the 'We are all Khaled Said' Facebook group, Wael Ghonim, had been arrested. He was blindfolded for 12 days and interrogated. After pressure mounted for his release, he was freed from prison. Hours later he appeared on national television to explain his ordeal, crying as he insisted 'I am not a traitor' and 'I love my country'. In response to people praising his actions, he replied: 'I am no hero. The heroes are the ones who were in the streets. The heroes are the ones that got beaten up. The heroes are the ones [who were] shot and arrested and put their lives in danger, I am no hero.' When the presenter showed him pictures of people who had died while he had been incarcerated, he left the set in tears.

The responses on Twitter reflected the impact of the broadcast. 'Everyone is crying. Everyone,' wrote 'Nevinezaki', mirrored by 'Sandmonkey' writing, 'Millions will go to Tahrir tomorrow, millions'. Perhaps the importance of the appearance was summed up by 'Mennaamr' who, shortly after midnight, wrote: 'I've been terrified the revolution would fade but Ghonim made that impossible. Thank you for being one hell of an inspiration to everyone.'

The next day lived up to its promise. Not only were there massive demonstrations but the number and militancy of strikes grew, too. On 9 February, the nascent anti-government trade unions finally began to move as one and threatened a general strike if Mubarak did not stand down. In so doing they added a new aspect of Counterpower to the mix – Economic Counterpower. Two days later, Mubarak resigned. In the words of independent trade unionist Kamal Abbas: 'No one believed that our revolution could succeed against the strongest dictatorship in the region. But in 18 days the revolution achieved the victory of the people. When the [organized] working class of Egypt joined the revolution on 9 and 10 February, the dictatorship was doomed and the victory of the people became inevitable.'[14]

The Twitter feeds of 11 February communicate the joy of the protesters in Tahrir Square that night. 'Ppl are going crazy, screaming and running', reported 'Monasosh'. Hossam el-Hamalawy wrote, 'I can't recall how many times we thought we're about to b massacred & our revolution'd be squashed. Still the will of the people prevailed'. Gigi Ibrahim was overcome with emotion, tweeting simply, 'I can't stop crying. I've never been more proud in my life'. Long after midnight 'Monasosh' tweeted again, 'This is where it all started on #Jan25 when we declared our demands ppl thought we were mad. Look where madness got us.'

As I write, the Consolidation Stage of the revolution is far from over. There have been some notes of warning sounded. For example, Hossam el-Hamalawy has blogged his concern that the 'the same IMF and "economists" who screwed our economy with their neoliberal recommendations from 1992 onwards, are coming out again today to congratulate us, promising us a bright future, as long as we stick to their policies, again!'[15] Gigi Ibrahim is every bit as determined that the revolution should not be co-opted: 'The main part of any revolution has to be socio-economic emancipation for the citizens of a country; if you want to eliminate corruption or stop vote-buying, then you have to give people decent salaries, make them aware of their rights and not leave them in dire economic need.'[13] Many Egyptians are speaking of continuous revolution, as protests continue – including in Tahrir Square – emphasizing that all of the demands have not yet been met.

One of the most frequent epithets attached to the Egyptian revolution is that it was an uprising instigated by the internet. Ibrahim is dismissive of such claims: 'Yes, we used the internet to communicate and spread information, but if the struggle wasn't there, if the people didn't take to the streets, if the factories didn't shut down, if workers didn't go on strike, none of this would have happened.' In this statement are encapsulated the major elements of Counterpower – including the Economic Counterpower of strike action and the Physical Counterpower of the action on the streets. The Idea Counterpower of communicating alternative ideas cannot be underestimated either. As Hossam el-Hamalawy puts it: 'In dictatorship, independent journalism by default becomes a form of activism. The spread of information is essentially an act of agitation'.[16]

The revolution delayed

The stories of events in Tunisia and Egypt were quick to inspire campaigners elsewhere. The protests spread, as the people of Algeria, Bahrain, Jordan, Kuwait, Morocco, Oman, Libya and Yemen rose up in different ways. Leaders fearful of losing power offered concessions. Protesters in Algeria won the lifting of a state of emergency that had been in place for almost 20 years. Protests in Yemen and Sudan have prompted existing rulers to promise not to stand again. The King of Jordan fired his entire cabinet, including the prime minister. Workers in Saudi Arabia and Oman have been promised better wages and conditions, while in Kuwait the Emir has given every citizen $4,000 in an attempt to suppress dissent.[17] Such desperate measures to maintain hold of power have been accompanied by physical repression of protests. Saudi Arabia even dispatched a 1,500-strong security force to Bahrain to quell the unrest there.

A downside to the way that events in Egypt have been reported is that a belief has been sown that if social movements simply occupy the streets for long enough, change will follow. Yet the stories in this book suggest that if the interests of those in power are not threatened – especially through the use of Economic or Physical Counterpower – the likelihood of rulers voluntarily giving up power altogether is small. Indeed, the substantial concessions that were elicited can be seen as a method to prevent the protests from escalating.

One country that has tried a different form of Counterpower is Libya – where the Idea Counterpower of demonstrations quickly turned to the Physical Counterpower of an armed uprising counterbalanced by the organized military power of the Libyan government. When NATO intervened on behalf of the rebels, it may have strengthened the movement's Physical Counterpower to some extent but also strengthened the Idea Power of Muammar Qadafi's government, enabling him to cast his opponents as pawns of the West. As Arab Spring turned to Arab Summer, the parties remained in stalemate.

However, it may be that many of the protest movements across the region are only in the Consciousness Stage – perhaps comparable to Egypt in the early 2000s. Like those earlier protests, the demonstrations in many countries have been met with physical repression. But it is possible that this wave of dissent will sow the seeds for something much bigger. It may take many Arab Springs to get there. But I hope that they will.

The legend of the Arab Spring is being felt beyond the Middle East. In Spain, thousands of people have occupied central squares, mirrored in cities across Europe. In London, too, protests have been organized in emulation of events in Cairo. It was at one such protest that the first words of the next and final section of this book were written.

1 Although this part of the legend is denied by the Tunisian authorities. **2** *The Independent*, 'I Have Lost My Son but I am Proud of What he Did', nin.tl/kK9vhL **3** All tweets in this chapter can be found in Nadia Idle and Alex Nunns (eds), *Tweets from Tahrir*, OR Books, 2011. **4** Azza Khalil, 'Demands Grow in Egypt for Social Justice and Democracy', in Francois Polet (ed), *State of Resistance: Popular Struggles in the Global South*, Zed, London, 2007. **5** Hossam el-Hamalawy, 'Egypt's Revolution has been 10 Years in the Making', nin.tl/mCQuto **6** arabawy.org, 'Police Abort Mahalla Strike', nin.tl/ksFVum **7** Although this is not the case for all activists. Hossam el-Hamalawy, for example, names the Palestinian struggle as the major source of inspiration rather than Gene Sharp, 'whose name I first heard in my life only in February after we toppled Mubarak already'. **8** Although not part of the beginning of the mobilization, the oppositional forces also included the Muslim Brotherhood on the right. **9** Al-Jazeera, 'Egyptians protest over minimum wage', nin.tl/jo3vOu and *New Internationalist*, 'Interview with Gigi Ibrahim', nin.tl/kgJ8KX **10** *Red Pepper*, 'Interview with Gigi Ibrahim', Apr/May 2011. **11** Al-Jazeera, *Egypt: Seeds of Change*, nin.tl/jcps5p **12** *London Review of Books*, 'Why Tunis? Why Cairo', nin.tl/lUA5pm **13** *New Internationalist*, op cit. **14** South Carolina Green Party, 'Egyptian union leader Kamal Abbas in solidarity with Wisconsin workers', nin.tl/jSPyxe **15** arabawy.org, 'This revolution actually serves Israel as well', nin.tl/mD7Qcn **16** arabawy.org homepage. **17** *Red Pepper*, Apr/May 2011.

9
Conclusion: making change happen

'*We cannot say that in the process of revolution someone liberates someone else, nor yet that that someone liberates himself, but rather that human beings in communion liberate each other.*'

Paulo Freire

The writing of this book has been punctuated by protest. It began in the wake of a major day of action and it ends in the wake of one too. I started writing the first draft of this conclusion in London on 26 March 2011, sitting on the steps of Nelson's Column, scribbling in my notebook and watching the activity in Trafalgar Square below. All day, different groups had shown their disapproval for the British government's cuts program in different ways. Up to half a million people marched from the Embankment to Hyde Park to be addressed by trade union leaders. Student groups organized unofficial feeder marches. Activists from UK Uncut peacefully occupied businesses accused of tax dodging. A small group with their faces covered smashed some windows. And then there was the protest in Trafalgar Square.

Calling the protest 'Turn Trafalgar into Tahrir', the participants pledged to stay the night. In many ways the atmosphere was that of an after-party, complete with dancing to sound-systems and samba bands. A large number of people were of school age. On the other side of the square, a group of older people gave speeches. I left as evening fell to write up my notes. By the time I arrived home, the television was reporting that the protest had erupted into violence. A spokesperson from the police was interviewed, calling the protesters 'mindless yobs' and declaring that 'they don't care who they hurt' – implying that people were being 'kettled' there by police to stop them from attacking members of the public. Yet the first-hand accounts and videos uploaded to the internet told a different story. Police were violently removing protesters.

The media reported that 149 arrestees had been charged after the day's protests.[1] It didn't take long to emerge that 145 of them were in fact UK Uncut activists who had rather politely occupied the upmarket shop Fortnum and Mason in protest at tax dodging. As one person inside the shop wrote afterwards: 'We sang songs and held our banners and shoppers seemed to be quite amused by the whole thing.'[2] The protesters were arrested despite assurances that they would not be. After taking them to the cells, police confiscated activists' clothes and phones. They traveled home the next day in plastic jump suits.

For a week afterwards the blogosphere exploded with debate. Should we have just marched from A to B? Did the nonviolent civil disobedience take away from the message or add to it? Will the window smashing isolate the movement? Does campaigning make a difference anyway? In many ways it was different only in the detail from the questions that characterize discussion in campaigning movements across the world and throughout history. I am sorry to say that this conclusion will not resolve those debates. What it does do is provide a view in response to each of the most frequent questions that come up. OK, here we go.

Are 'insider' or 'outsider' methods more effective?

Probably the most fundamental question in political organizing is whether 'insider' methods of talking to government or 'outsider' methods like protests, strikes and occupations are more effective. This is sometimes characterized as the divide between advocates of reform or revolution.

Almost every campaign group in this book began by asking nicely. The Indian National Congress even went so far as to support the First World War, only to be rewarded by the repressive Rowlatt Act. They learned the hard way that if you jump into bed with the government you'll most likely get screwed.

But there is an important difference between begging and negotiating. As manuals on trade-union organizing make clear, constructive negotiation can only take place if the parties enter talks as equals. This is only possible with the use of Counterpower. Thus the fact that Churchill complained about the 'half-naked fakir' Gandhi parleying 'on equal terms with the representative of the king-emperor' implies that the time to bargain was right. Similarly, as noted in Chapter 5, the fact that the apartheid regime saw fit to open talks with a man serving a life prison sentence is testament to the powerful effect of the 'outsider' Counterpower of the wider movement.

In the end, though, India achieved its independence, apartheid was ended in South Africa and universal suffrage was introduced in Britain following steps by élites to stop more radical alternatives from taking hold. A successful campaign is an unfinished revolution.

Do demonstrations work?

Another major debate is about the role of protests that simply march from A to B. Some people see it as necessary for movement building, while others see it as a failed tactic. Looking at history, both have a point. Every successful movement surveyed in this book used the public demonstration as one of its tactics. But none of the movements examined in this book was successful through demonstrations alone.

Three of the biggest demonstrations of the last decade in the UK were the anti-war march on 15 February 2003, the Make Poverty History march on 2 July 2005 and the 'March for the Alternative' on 26 March 2011. It is important to note that every one of these processions was followed by marked swings in public opinion. Disillusion with the Iraq War passed 50 per cent *three days after* the February 2003 march. Concern for global poverty peaked in July 2005. The Conservatives fell 10 points behind in the polls in early April 2011, just days after the mass march against their program.

One explanation for this is that the very act of building for a demonstration gives grassroots activists an excuse to talk to family, friends and strangers about the issues they care about. Whether they attend or not, those people will then see the demonstration reported in the media and recall the conversation they had. In the case of very large marches, it is possible that a majority of people in the country know at least someone who took part – thus making the arguments more personal. Another possible reason – complementary to the others – is that the sense of togetherness fostered by the street demonstration reassures waverers that they are not alone in their doubts. This can be built upon as the perspectives of campaigners make their way into the press, thereby amending the media narrative. The demonstration then can primarily be seen as a form of Idea Counterpower.

The problem comes when movements see demonstrations *only* as a form of Idea Counterpower. They are better seen as a demonstration of *intent* – a warning that if the powers that be do not cede power, the people will claim it themselves with every form of Counterpower available to them. I think of demonstrations as comparable to the All-Blacks performing the *haka* before a rugby game: it is designed both to prepare for the confrontation ahead and to give the opponent an impression of what the movement could be capable of.[3] Of course, on occasion, the very fact that people have organized means that they win some concessions. Saul Alinsky has an explanation for this when he says 'the threat is usually more terrifying than the thing itself'.[4] But the demonstration cannot be the be-all-and-end-all of the campaign.

How do we decide which tactics to use?

Some strategists begin their planning by mapping where they consider power to be and then orienting their campaigns towards influencing those people. For the pursuit of small-scale change within the dominant power structures, this is a logical approach. But to effect fundamental change, such an approach is somewhat limited. Of course, recognizing where power lies in society is an important step but the next step is to look at the potential Counterpower available to the movement so that the oppressed can claim power for themselves.

There is no definitive list of all the possible methods of Counterpower. In *The Politics of Nonviolent Action*, Gene Sharp lists 198 different methods. Since the invention of the internet, there are now many more. If you are in a group, one way to do this is to split into two teams to see who can come up with the most methods. It is then possible to look through the lists and ask which would count as Economic Counterpower, which as Physical Counterpower and which as Idea Counterpower.

Another method is to engage in a game of 'campaigns chess'. One person plays the part of the target, the other the part of the movement. They take it in turns to say how they would defeat the other one. For example, the person being the movement might begin by saying 'I would send you a letter', to which the target might respond 'I would ignore your letter', leading the movement player to say 'I would turn up with placards', to which the target might respond by saying 'I would smear you in the press' and so on. The player that wins is usually the one who (consciously or not) uses the power they have and targets the weaknesses of their opponent. In this respect it is very like a game of chess.

But there is an important difference. Whereas in chess the players start out with an equal number of pieces, campaigning movements almost always start out with fewer resources than their opponents. The challenge for the movement then is to work out what the sources of the target's power are. Its idea power might be based on promotion of a certain ideology or popularity of a certain brand. Its economic power might be based on certain transport links, having enough staff or the ability to sell things. Its physical power is usually based on its economic and idea power. Plotting the opponent's strengths and weaknesses will help campaigners exploit the weak points of their targets.

In *Rules for Radicals*, Saul Alinsky discusses the ideas of blocking toilets at airports and getting people to buy, and then return, goods at department stores. In this book we saw examples of this played out on a larger scale: for example, the miners' strike and coking plant blockades of the 1970s in Britain that won a 20-per-cent pay rise for the workers and contributed to the downfall of the Conservative government. The Bolivian road blockades of the early 2000s first helped to get rid of Bechtel and then contributed to the downfall of the rightwing president. In all of these cases, campaigners identified what was necessary for power institutions to thrive, then asked themselves whether their organization could creatively intervene in a bottleneck. If they could, they did.

Sometimes, however, bottlenecks are to the benefit of the *haves*. For example, the mainstream media could be thought of as an information bottleneck which, for a number of reasons,[5] tends to favor the perspectives of the *haves* over those of the *have nots*. Changing power relations tend to be reflected in changing press coverage. But, while the movement is still discriminated against, campaigners often create their own media. This is plain to see from the radical unstamped press of the 18th century, to the anti-war 'zines of the 1960s and the radical blogs and journals of today. All of these alternative media sources serve to bypass the information bottleneck and to build Idea Counterpower.

If there is more than one organization working on a certain issue, a useful method can be to plot out what needs to happen and what is happening already. This is a good way to identify where you or your group are best placed to intervene – either to strengthen an existing activity or to start a new one which complements the work that others are doing. It may be that one organization is not best placed to organize Idea Counterpower, Economic Counterpower *and* Physical Counterpower. But, as established, a movement *as a whole* has the best chance of success if it uses all three – or, better still, uses a combination of them to undermine the economic, physical and idea power of the government.

Must our actions be acceptable to the mainstream media?

A concern for many campaigners is that certain actions might isolate potential supporters and make the government less likely to listen to the movement's point of view. I have heard this argued even when the government has already openly said that it will disregard the views of the movement anyway.

Sometimes this is the case even if the movement is mainly using Idea Counterpower – as in the case of the media hysteria against many anti-war campaigners during World War One. But had the anti-war campaigners of that time attempted to campaign within the 'frame' of patriotism and nationalism, it is likely they could have been even less successful than they were, and would never have helped create the meme for an alternative frame based on justice and peace. Transferred to today, recent studies suggest that green and anti-poverty campaigners would be more successful if they helped to build notions of justice and community through their communications, rather than inadvertently reinforcing worldviews based on individualism.[6]

The debate about media perception is often most fraught when debating whether or not to engage in acts of Physical Counterpower. Some of the most cleverly designed acts of Physical Counterpower double up with Idea Counterpower to win the sympathy of the mainstream media – the maiden Greenpeace voyage, for example, or more recently the shop occupations organized by UK Uncut. But it is not usually the case. In general, when a movement adopts a more militant approach, it suffers at the hands of the newspapers – at least at first.

Yet, whether reported favorably or not, one of the effects of some groups using Physical Counterpower is to make reformist/insider groups appear more moderate. The German regime handing power to the Social Democrats to keep the Spartacists at bay is a good example of this. So too are the negotiations that took place with mainstream green groups in the UK after protesters occupied the trees at proposed road-building sites.

Another possible outcome of the use of Physical Counterpower is that, while it might play badly for the media image of the protesters involved, it can be even worse for the target. For example, the first major escalation of the UK anti-cuts campaign came in 2010 when a group broke away from a 50,000-strong student march and occupied the Conservative Party's headquarters. All evening, the television showed pictures of students smashing windows, storming police lines and daubing slogans on the building. Polls after the event showed that the public generally disapproved. However, just the following day, the governing Conservative Party fell to second place in the opinion polls, and remained there for the succeeding months. Whether this was coincidental or due to the main demonstration is a matter that would require further research. What it does indicate, though, is that it did not undermine the cause, and may even have boosted it as it precipitated a new wave of protest in the weeks that followed.

When is it right to escalate?

Finding the right time to escalate will probably form one of the most difficult decisions of all. Bill Moyer argues that, in the early stage of campaigns, participants should use mainly constitutional means – not because they will make a difference, but to show how the *haves* are preventing the democratic system from operating democratically.[7] Similarly, Saul Alinsky advises that fundamental change only takes place when the people feel 'so futureless in the prevailing system that they are willing to let go of the past and chance the future'.[4] But the wait cannot be too long. There is a case to be made that it is not confrontation but failure to confront which isolates movements.

A key factor in winning support for the move to the Confrontation Stage is confrontation itself. This is clearly to be seen in the campaign for the vote, when events like the arrest of Thomas Spence and the suffragettes shouting at Manchester's Free Trade Hall conveyed the message that the game was changing. The publicity awarded to these new kinds of responses encouraged more people to attain Critical Consciousness and join the movement themselves. This tallies with Joe Slovo's view that 'until the new type of action is started, it is doubtful whether political mobilization and organization can be developed beyond a certain point... a demonstration of the liberation movement's capacity to meet and sustain the struggle in a new way is in itself a vital way of attracting organized allegiance and support.'[8]

For some, any escalation will be too soon. When the US civil-rights campaigners occupied the lunch counters, the suffragettes jumped up at a political meeting and the road protesters occupied the proposed road site at Twyford, they were all condemned by some of their elders. But history has proved that their timing was right.

Do the ends justify the means?

This book has argued that most successful movements use Idea Counterpower, Economic Counterpower and Physical Counterpower to undermine the power of regimes. As seen in the decolonization of India, civil rights in the US and the toppling of dictators in Benin and Poland, Counterpower does not have to use weapons to be successful.

Not everything reported in the media as violence can rightly be thought of as violent – a case in point being damage to property. Some case studies from this book help to clarify the distinction. Take the Jesuit priests who later became known as part of the Catonsville Nine, who burned draft files during the Vietnam War. Their act certainly caused damage to property but most people would say that it was not violent. Neither could we consider the activists who cut fences at Fairford Airbase in order to sabotage B-52 jets as violent. As is evident from these examples, there is a clear distinction between nonviolent civil disobedience involving damage to property, and violence.

However, some of the actions described in this book were unmistakably violent. The Bolshevik coup in 1917, Ho Chi Minh's armed resistance in Vietnam and the actions of Umkhonto We Sizwe in southern Africa are all cases in point. To different extents, violent tactics played a part in creating change in those respective countries. An important question to be asked, though, is what *kind* of change violence is capable of achieving. Looking again at the cases mentioned, it would seem that, the greater the role of violence in social change, the lesser the democracy of the post-transition settlement.

In contrast, a recent study of 67 different revolutions found that levels of democratic rights were far higher in countries that had used nonviolent methods to achieve democracy.[9] Another piece of research, looking at the myriad revolutions in Africa between 1989 and 1994, concludes that democratization occurred most frequently in countries that liberalized following mass political protests, rather than through bloody revolution or coups.[10]

An explanation for why this might be is provided by the earlier work of Gene Sharp. He argues that violent revolutions born of coups and wars lead to the state centralizing power and acting with greater brutality. Sharp cites the hierarchy necessary for successful armed struggle as a key reason for this, as it tends to be reflected in post-transitional societies. Coupled with this is the assertion that social approval for violence as a tool of political change legitimizes violence against and by post-liberation governments, leading to greater state repression in response.[11]

On the other hand, in nonviolent movements the power of the leadership is weak and the power of the membership is strong. Leaders of nonviolent struggles have no power to cut off arms supplies to or shoot their critics. Furthermore, if the movement is to be successful, it must be self-reliant, as the leadership may spend substantial time behind bars. As a result, changes won through nonviolent struggle are accompanied by the capacity to defend those changes nonviolently against future threats.

Nonviolent change is both possible and more likely to bring about real revolutions of power than coups or civil war. Furthermore, following the argument that struggle based on Counterpower never ends, violent struggle could lead to perpetual violence. The means *are* the ends.

Does campaigning make a difference?

The stories in this book show that campaigning can and does make a difference – and that it does so through the use of Counterpower. Even those campaigns that failed in their primary objectives on the whole led to positive changes in other ways, whether planned for or not.

Some people have argued that campaigning doesn't make a difference and that social change is simply a by-product of other events. But while external events are hugely important, they are the context to change rather than the drivers of it. The First World War was the backdrop to revolution in Russia. The Second World War preceded the liberation of India. The end of the Cold War helped spur revolutions across eastern Europe and sub-Saharan Africa. But while major economic or political shake-ups help create the conditions for change by 'disorganizing' societies, it is sustained pressure that helps shape what direction society takes. None of these changes would have happened without the longstanding campaigns that preceded them. It is not only the redistribution of power that can happen following such external events. As Naomi Klein shows in *The Shock Doctrine*, the neoliberal right is highly adept at taking advantage of wars, economic crises and even natural disasters to consolidate power with the few.

The change created by campaigning can manifest itself in a number of ways. Very occasionally, the target apologizes and changes their policy, or even stands down altogether. More frequently, governing élites deny that the movement has had any effect but then quietly make changes at a later date, or try to co-opt the movement by claiming that they agreed all along. Most often – as with the Defiance Campaign in South Africa, the Salt March in India and the Chartists' activities in Britain – élites do not change but the movement emerges stronger and better able to work for wider-scale redistribution of power.

Whether feudal, capitalist or communist, élites have promoted the view that change has stopped happening as a shroud to disguise the over-concentration of power. Neoliberals in the US in the 1990s such as Francis Fukuyama claimed that the world had already reached the 'end of history'. Some declared the Soviet Union a utopia. As has been quoted, as far back as 1794, Judge Braxfield declared that 'The British constitution is the best that ever was since the creation of the world and it is not possible to make it better'. But it is always possible to make things better. Every time élites abuse their power, people use Counterpower to challenge them.

This is not a theory confined to books. Right now, across the world, people are using their Counterpower to challenge injustice. I hope you will be part of the next chapter.

1 BBC, Anti-cuts Demo Unrest Sees 149 Charged, bbc.co.uk/news/uk-12876705
2 Political Dynamite, a view from a UK UNCUT-ter, nin.tl/keez4U **3** Thanks to Annette Davis for introducing me to this analogy. **4** Saul Alinsky, *Rules for Radicals: A Pragmatic Primer for Realistic Radicals,* Vintage, Toronto, 1971. **5** See Nick Davies, *Flat Earth News,* Chatto & Windus, 2008, and Noam Chomsky, *Media Control,* Seven Stories Press, New York, 2002. **6** See WWF and others, *Common Cause,* nin.tl/mptaYs **7** Bill Moyer, *The Movement Action Plan,* 1987 nin.tl/l16Hkz **8** Joe Slovo (et al), *Southern Africa: The New Politics of Revolution,* Penguin, London, 1976. **9** Adrian Karatnycky and Peter Ackerman, *How Freedom Is Won,* Freedom House, Washington, 2005. freedomhouse.org/uploads/special_report/29.pdf
10 Michael Bratton and Nicolas Van de Walle, *Democratic Experiments in Africa: Regime Transitions in Comparative Perspective,* Cambridge University Press, 1997.
11 Gene Sharp, *Waging Nonviolent Struggle: 20th Century Practice and 21st Century Potential,* Porter Sargeant, Boston, 2005.

Index